sense of purpose

to your plan; to deal with

pressure, thrive on it, and

make it your own; to carve

away the distractions that

slow us all down; and,

perhaps most important,

to keep going after you

lose the biggest race of

your life.

Because you will. I did

several times. **"**

SLAYING THE DRAGON

MICHAEL JOHNSON

SLAYING THE DRAGO

ReganBooks
An Imprint of HarperCollinsPublishers

HOW TO TURN YOUR SMALL STEPS TO GREAT FEATS

HarperCollins books may be purchased for educational, business, or sales promotional use. For information please write: Special Markets Department, HarperCollins Publishers, Inc., 10 East 53rd Street, New York, NY 10022.

FIRST EDITION

Designed by Elina D. Nudelman

ISBN 0-06-039218-5

96 97 98 99 00 ❖/RRD 10 9 8 7 6 5 4 3 2 1

TO MY PARENTS, PAUL AND RUBY JOHNSON,
WHO ARE *MY* ROLE MODELS

CONTENTS

FOREWORD by Muhammad Ali   ix

ACKNOWLEDGMENTS   xi

INTRODUCTION   xiii

PART I:
QUALIFYING

DREAMS   3

DISCIPLINE   25

DISAPPOINTMENT   49

PART II:
TRIALS

ACHIEVEMENT   77

AWARENESS   109

ANGUISH   133

PART III:
THE GAMES

PERSEVERANCE   **157**

PRESSURE   **179**

PERFORMANCE   **201**

EPILOGUE   **221**

FOREWORD
by Muhammad Ali

The 1996 Olympic Games in Atlanta were very special to me, not only because I was selected to light the torch that signaled the start of the Olympics that year, but also because I was given the opportunity to meet the newest generation of greatest athletes ever to bless this earth. One of those athletes was Michael Johnson. Michael made Olympic history when he won gold in both the 200- and 400-meter dashes. Never before in the history of the Olympics had any single sprinter accomplished this feat.

I watched the 200-meter event in the quiet of my Atlanta hotel room. I knew Michael Johnson's name because of my five-year-old son's infatuation with Michael's past feats, but I did not yet know the man. As I watched Michael move closer to the finish line, I wondered how a man like that learns to become so fast and fluid that he almost appears surreal. Immediately, my thoughts turned to my own sport, boxing, and to echoes of the comments fans had used to describe my past performances in the ring. At that moment, I was struck by one thought: You reach the finish line one step at a time, one day at a time, and with the understanding that it will take many steps and many days to ensure you get there first. It was the same course I pursued when I became an Olympic Gold Medalist and three-time heavyweight boxing champion of the world. And it is as timeless as the lesson it teaches all new seekers of their own unique challenges: You achieve your goal one step at a time, focused and diligent, always moving forward.

In today's fast-paced society where athletes regularly draw multimillion-dollar paychecks, we sometimes forget the long hours of practice and work it takes for an athlete to become successful. Truthfully speaking, it never happens overnight. Hard work, perfect practice, and dedication to the goal of becoming better at your "sport" are just a few of the steps it takes to become a Michael Johnson, a Muhammad Ali, a Barbra Streisand, a Steven Spielberg, or a Bill Gates.

It works for everyone, not just superstar athletes. As you read Michael Johnson's inspired words, you will learn the skills you need, one step at a time, to go out and slay your own dragons.

ACKNOWLEDGMENTS

This book—as well as the achievements and methods described in it—would not have been possible without the contributions, examples, and support of many people.

I'd like to thank my parents, Paul and Ruby, for shaping and molding me and for their constant love and support. I am grateful to my brother, Paul Jr., who is also my best friend and who understands me without ever being judgmental; to my sisters, Regina, Cheryl, and Deidre, who have always been there for me and who have kept me honest and humble; and to my grandparents, Lee and Ida Grant, for the sacrifices they made for all of us.

I am indebted to my coach, Clyde Hart, a great teacher who has been responsible for my development in so many ways, and to my strength coach, Danny Brabham. I also want to thank my agent, manager, and friend, Brad Hunt, who has taught me so much; his staff at Gold Medal Management—Gigi and Janny—for their hard work; and my assistant, Robin Jones. Thanks also to my old friend Ray Crockett for being supportive and believing in me when others didn't, and to Mike Powell, director of photography at Allsport USA, who has covered my international career from the beginning.

This book came about because Judith Regan understood that I didn't want to write just another sports book. I am grateful to her and to the hardworking editors and production team at ReganBooks, including Todd Silverstein, Kristin Kiser, Jane Hardick, Elina Nudelman, Linda Dingler, Joe Rutt, and Susan Kosko. I am also grateful to David Morey and Marty Stern. Thanks finally to Jess Walter, who helped me put this together, and to his researcher, Bonnie Harris Hayes.

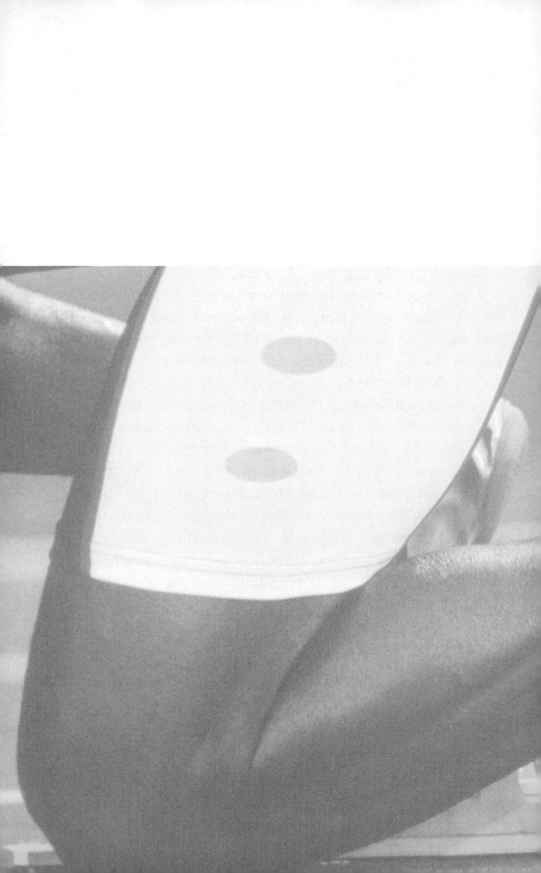

INTRODUCTION

It wasn't much of a stumble

really—more of a misstep, a flinch.

I surged from the blocks, legs churning, chewing track before my mind even had time to hear the gun and think "Go!"—like a pilot in rough takeoff evaluating all the systems and gauges and finding his craft running smoothly, except for that stumble, which was gone before I could identify it, when I was suddenly breaking through the curve like I was slung around it, arms pumping and the checklist running through my mind in the time it takes to blink: Hold low at first—check. Dig through the first few strides—check. And then fire upright, allow my power to take over, and then run like I always run, easily and strongly, so that this time everything felt perfect and I sliced the air in a pair of 2-ounce gold shoes and a uniform that felt no different than skin—and except for the exhilaration in my chest and in my head, I was a sleek, powerful machine. A perfect machine.

And yet . . .

There had been the stumble, the briefest shudder, step three to be exact. Imperceptible to anyone but me.

The finish line seemed to reach out and grab *me*, pull me toward it. I knew the race had been fast when I crossed, knew the record was gone when I looked over my shoulder, as other runners were still finishing, and that's when I saw the clock: 19 seconds and 32 hundredths. I had beaten my own world record by nearly a third of a second—something like a long weekend in sprinter time, where tenths of a second separate good seasons from bad ones. Nineteen-point-thirty-two! My arms flew open in disbelief and everything dissolved in a rush of camera flashes and congratulations, cheers and the powerful sense that I had done something truly special at the Olympic Games in Atlanta.

You must understand, I am not by nature a day-dreamer. I try to control those parts of my life that can be controlled, to plan everything that I want to happen down to the most insignificant detail. I traffic in a world in which fractions of a second separate success and failure, so I'd visualized the 1996 Olympics down to the millisecond. I'd crafted a decade of dreams into ambitions, refined ambitions into goals, and finally hammered goals into plans. There were countless repetitions in the weight room and intervals on the

1995 World Championships, Göteborg, Sweden.

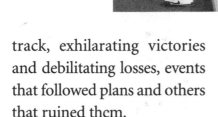

track, exhilarating victories and debilitating losses, events that followed plans and others that ruined them.

A decade! Ten years of my life leading to this achievement: gold medal in the 400 meters and gold medal in the 200 meters, the first man ever to win Olympic gold in those two very different races. It had all gone according to plan with two exceptions.

One was the stumble. The other was 19.32.

Ten years ago, I had run the same distance in 21 seconds, good for a high school athlete but well short of world class. A decade of tireless work and complete dedication had earned me little more than 1.5 seconds. A second and a half! That was the difference between being mediocre and being the fastest in the world. Barely time for a breath, an inhale and exhale. No more than a whisper from perfection.

Perfection. In the end, I suppose that's why I run, not just for the other runners on the track or for the people in the stands or watching on television, not just because of the pressure inside or out, certainly not just because of the records or the desire to make history. Those things are all part of it, of course, but the reason is larger than any of them. I just wonder sometimes: Is it possible to run a perfect race?

I broke my own world record in the 1996 Olympics' 200-meter final by one of the largest margins in history—almost a third of a second.

There is a saying among some athletes that after you have stared long enough into the dragon's eyes, there is nothing left to do but slay the dragon. For each of us, that dragon is the thing closest to the center of our lives. It is our core, our ambition, and our joy. For me, it is the perfect race.

I mean, I had just run 23 miles per hour, like a car through the suburbs, faster than any human being has ever been tracked. I had beaten the best runners in the world in two very different races, in the face of towering pressure. And yet there was that stumble and a million questions that it posed as I prepared to write this book.

How much faster could I have gone without the stumble? Is it possible that we can always go farther and higher? Can I always go faster?

Success is found in much smaller portions than most people realize, achieved through the tiniest gradations, not unlike the

split-second progress of a sprinter. A hundredth of a second here or sometimes a tenth there can determine the fastest man in the world. Two cars might separate the best salesman from the worst. One misspelling might determine the valedictorian. At times, we live our lives on a paper-thin edge that barely separates greatness from mediocrity and success from failure.

That sliver of performance is where you will find the rewards that come from a sprinter's training, from the confidence, discipline, and focus that I have honed my entire career. Life is often compared to a marathon, but I think it is more like being a sprinter: long stretches of hard work punctuated by brief moments in which we are given the opportunity to perform at our best.

I've heard a lot recently about being a role model, from the media, from my friends, and once from a woman who was put out when I asked her to wait a few minutes for an autograph. I happen to disagree with our culture's habit of creating instant role models out of athletes. And yet I am honored to be in that position. I come from a family of teachers and I have learned a great deal from others: from my family, from my

coaches, from other athletes, and from a few heroes of my own, people like Jesse Owens and Muhammad Ali, who have inspired me through their example, through incredible victories and terrifying losses, through lives that were even more brilliant in their fullness than they were in their individual achievements.

To me, that's the ultimate responsibility and challenge of being a role model—not to sign autographs in a timely fashion or to live a stainless life, but to offer up a life or a philosophy, flaws and all, to help other people negotiate their own way. That's what I hope to do in this book.

So I have not set out to write about how you can be an Olympic champion or how you can break world records. Those are rarely attainable goals and, honestly, there are more worthy ones for most people. Especially in the beginning. My main goal ten years ago was to go to college. Yet the Atlanta Olympics would never have happened for me without that first goal. It is the same with you. You'll never know how far you can go until you shave off that first hundredth of a second, until you run ceaselessly toward the edge.

1996 Olympic Games, Atlanta, Georgia.

And so this is a book about how to identify what you really want and how to get there; to set goals based upon realism and confidence; to work with discipline and resolve; to learn from the requisite failures and the too-early successes; to achieve a clarity of focus and a sense of purpose; to stick to your plan; to deal with pressure, thrive on it, and make it your own; to carve away the distractions that slow us all down; and, perhaps most important, to keep going after you lose the biggest race of your life. Because you will. I did several times.

I will show you what I did after each of those terrible losses: how to retool your machine, regain your focus, and find another biggest race. And another. And another.

Finally, I will show you what I have only now realized: Even in the best race there will always be a slight stumble, a shudder, a hitch, always room for a hundredth of a second improvement. That is the great thing about being a human being. You can always go just a little bit faster.

I wish I could teach you how to achieve perfection, how to slay the dragon every time. Instead, I hope to show you something far more valuable: how to chase it.

1996 U.S. Olympic Trials, Atlanta, Georgia.

PART I:
QUALIFYING

DREAMS

DISCIPLINE

DISAPPOINTMENT

DREAMS

50-YARD DASH

An inch of time is an inch of gold.
— CHINESE PROVERB

I guess I've always loved to

go fast. Mixed in with all the other memories of childhood are exhilarating images of speed—foot races up and down the street, squinting into a self-made headwind, watching the scenery blur on both sides, and the explosive feeling of being faster than someone else. I ran everywhere, as kids do, and rode my bike when I realized that it was an even faster way to travel. That was followed by the go-cart my father built in his focused, mechanical way, which brought even more speed and was the only thing I could think of when someone asked me, after Atlanta, what it felt like to run that fast.

It was, I said, like driving that old go-cart.

I believe that's where our best inspiration comes from, not from the sophisticated adult desires for power or prestige or money, but from the simple adolescent dreams: Run fast, jump high, be in love, have fun.

I'm lucky that I was young when I realized what I am chas-

ing—speed—the thing so close to my core that I'm willing to do all it takes to excel. If you are like most people, you might not find that essential desire, that core, until you're much older. You might never recognize it in yourself. We all know perfectly happy people in their fifties who say, "I don't know what I want to be when I grow up." I think that's incredibly healthy. There's no reason your chase can't change, your dreams adapt. When my running career is over, I plan to approach business with the same focus and energy, and when I marry and have children, I plan to invest the same joy and hard work in my family life. I will run tirelessly after something else when I "grow up."

Sometimes, though, our deepest dreams don't translate very well to the culture we live in. Not everyone thrives in athletics or business or education; not everyone craves the competitive sort of challenges that most of us face every day. That's OK. You can't force yourself to be a climber in the office if it's not the thing that sparks your mind and heart. But you can use the methods that work in athletics and business to take better control of your life. I believe the path that leads through self-discipline and order is the way to all sorts of diverse success and happiness, not just the way to winning.

For instance, I've thought a lot about my parents' motivation. They were intelligent, hardworking people—my mother a teacher, my father a truck driver—who took great pride in their careers. But their respective jobs had little to do with their cores, that essential place where inspiration comes from. I doubt my father expected to get rich from truck driving or that he dreamed of being the best truck driver ever.

My parents' dream was a big, successful, happy family and they worked at that the way other people might chase success in a law office or on the golf course. My father didn't just hope that his children would finish their homework or hope that we would take part in family vacations. Paul Johnson Sr. planned almost every detail

**The Johnsons, 1971.
Front row (from left): Deidre, Paul Jr., me. Back row (from left): Regina, Cheryl, Paul Sr.**

of every vacation. He set up guidelines for each of his kids and expected us to live our lives the same way. He constantly told us about the plan and challenged us to have our own when we came to him with things we wanted to do or accomplish. I admire him and my mother for that and for their preparation and hard work. I work hard, but it is for obvious goals: gold medals, world records, to make a living. My parents worked just as hard, harder sometimes (after all, there were five children), without the acclaim and the money. And they raised five happy, well-adjusted, bright college graduates: a teacher, a school counselor, a systems analyst, a special agent for the U.S. Department of Defense, and myself. (In fact, now that I think about it, I'm the only one who doesn't have a good, steady job.)

The Johnson men, from left to right: me, Paul Jr., and Paul Sr., 1969.

My father was one of those men who knew everything, could answer any question, and could fix anything. Knees sticking out from under some car, he could explain the workings of any machine ever built and give advice on any topic. People marvel at my self-confidence, but it is my father's confidence, and it comes from understanding the world around you and knowing that, in your world, things happen according to plan.

Too often we go into something like parenting without much thought or preparation. We think nothing of doing research on investments or scouring car lots for the best deal, but how many people do you know who actually *work* at parenting, who approach it with the same dedication they might a project at work or a class in school?

Mom and me on vacation at Pike's Peak, 1973.

We owe it to ourselves to approach everything in our lives that way.

And that's where a sprinter's training comes in. Imagine your life as a series of races, a strand of goals on the way to some larger accomplishment (usually far off and unfocused at first, like the Olympics). Connecting those smaller goals are training and plans, and the more refined you become, the closer you move to your ultimate goal—to fulfilling that core desire inside of yourself—the more you realize that the plans are the really important part, more important even than the goals.

Plans are the string holding the pearls together.

Your goals will become closer and closer together as you improve in your chosen area. I don't play very much golf, but I am told that lowering your score becomes progressively harder

1996 U.S. Olympic Trials, Atlanta, Georgia.

the more you play the game. It is that way with everything. When you begin to perform at higher levels, the only difference between winning and losing, between succeeding and failing, is the precision and preparation of your plans.

So, at the beginning of the season, I sit down and talk with my coach and with other people whose opinions I value. And I think about what I want to do that year. When I've identified specific goals, I write them down on a sheet of paper. Then I ask myself the old Paul Johnson Sr. question: "How are you going to do that?" That's when I connect the dots, stringing plans between those goals. This year, of course, my goal was to win Olympic gold medals in the 200 meters and the 400 meters, so I wrote that down.

But to get that far, I had to convince the Olympic committee to change the schedule so that heats for both races weren't held on the same day. I wrote that down as well. But first, I had to qualify for both events at the Olympic Trials. And before that, I had to be at peak sprinting performance and have increased stamina. And to get that far, I had to adjust my training schedule, sharpening it to improve my training to be able to run two very different races. And to do that . . . It goes on and on.

The point is that to improve incrementally, you must plan incrementally. And the best way to do that, to think it all through, to make sure you've missed nothing, is to write it down. A written goal is a contract with yourself and a constant reminder of all you still have to do. Having a record is vital; it's the first step in learning to put yourself on the hook, to being responsible to yourself.

It is also important to be specific and realistic when you set goals. I had been the number one–ranked runner in both the 200 and the 400 at different times in my career, and although

I'd only run both races in the same meet twice, I was in a better position than anyone else in the world to try winning both. That's being realistic.

I could easily have set more unrealistic goals. For instance, I have also run the 100 meters a few times in my career, and to have won all three races would have been incredible and unprecedented.

It also would have been impossible. Being realistic isn't settling for less than you're capable of doing; it isn't throwing away your dreams; it's simply acknowledging that, right now, you are incapable of doing some things. And it only works if you are able to take pride in the things you *can* do. My mother and one of my sisters are teachers and another sister is a school counselor. I admire them deeply and I imagine they dream of improving the lives of every student they come in contact with. But they are also realistic and know that they might not reach a few. Those are the times to revel in your successes, in the kids who make it.

The ability to set realistic goals only comes with experience and with the intimate knowledge of yourself that you acquire when you've worked hard and tested yourself. When in doubt, scale your goals back a little bit. If the aim is realistic, you'll get there soon enough.

Being specific is also key. At the beginning of the season, I charted the days, weeks, and months before the Atlanta games and figured out where I needed to be at each step along the way. That work is what tightens the focus on dreams and turns them into goals. I set as my pre-Olympic goals breaking 44 seconds in the 400 meters and breaking 20 in the 200. That way I knew I would have running times that would give me great chances of winning gold medals in both events (assuming

High School Graduation, 1986.

1994 USA Track &
Field Championships,
Knoxville, Tennessee.

everything else went according to plan). The importance of specificity can't be overstated. If I'd just set goals of running *well* in the 400 and the 200, the string connecting my goals would have been weakened and I might have settled for less.

That doesn't mean that if you don't reach each interval, each intermediate goal, you should give up on your larger goals. I never did break 44 seconds in the weeks before the Olympics. But I didn't panic and I didn't beat myself up. I just kept going, and in the end having a sub–44-second 400 as a goal—even an unachieved goal—helped me sharpen my training and win in Atlanta—where I set an Olympic 400-meter record of 43.49 seconds.

In all of this, I believe, the first step is knowing yourself. Cars are built now with on-board computers, small processors that constantly check and recheck the status of every operating part, that tell you when your door is open and even provide guidance systems to help you get where you're going. The on-board computer that you've been blessed with is a far more refined and impressive piece of machinery. However, in some people the computer has lost power through inactivity or its flashing messages have been ignored. I think that most of us have an innate sense of what we want and how to get there. You owe it to yourself to constantly check and recheck your computer, to assess the information coming from your mind, your body, and your core—the place where your dreams and ambitions lie. Your ambition may be an education. It may be getting your body in shape, losing weight, falling in love, battling cancer. It may be sculpture, poetry, or the 200-meter run. No matter what it is, you owe it to yourself to figure out what you are chasing.

And how you might catch it.

OUT OF THE BLOCKS

Ask yourself: "How do you plan to do that?"

Every time I burst into the house with some new dream or ambition ("I want to be an architect!"), my father would be waiting in the living room to ask me one simple question: "How do you plan to do that?" And it wasn't a rhetorical question. I was expected to list every step I planned to take, to research the amount of money I would earn, and to understand the kind of work required. Now, I have a voice inside my head that asks me the same thing before I begin. Find that voice in yourself.

OTHER VOICES

The question should be, is it worth trying to do, not can it be done.
—*Allard Lowenstein, twentieth-century American diplomat*

First, say to yourself what you would be; and then do what you have to do.
—*Epictetus, first-century Greek philosopher*

Nothing is impossible to a willing heart.
—*John Heywood, sixteenth-century English poet*

A man's worth is no greater than the worth of his ambitions.
—*Marcus Aurelius, second-century Roman emperor*

If you would hit the mark, you must aim a little above it; every arrow that flies feels the attraction of earth.
—*Henry Wadsworth Longfellow, nineteeth-century American poet*

WHAT I'M CHASING

THE 50-YARD DASH

I was a runner as a kid, but I wasn't "A Runner." Sure, we sprinted around the neighborhood, playing football in the afternoons after Cowboy games ("I'm Roger Staubach!" "I'm Drew Pearson!"), but I didn't envision myself as an Olympic sprinter and I didn't know any track athletes. I just ran because it was fun.

Kids always race. As the youngest of five children, I had no shortage of competitors when it came to racing. We raced to be first to the car, to be first to the house, to be first done with dinner, and we raced around a tidy working-class neighborhood where we didn't pay much attention to what color kids were or

how much money they had. We just ran.

I remember my first real race. I must have been ten years old and I believe we were running a 50-yard dash. Every summer we enrolled in the Dallas Parks and Recreation program, a sort of day camp at the park near our house in the Oak Cliff section of Dallas. There, we ran

First grade, 1974.

and played and worked on crafts until, one day, they took the fastest runners to another park for some kind of mini-Olympics. There wasn't a track at this larger park, just a few lanes strung through the grass and a finish line at the end. There were a bunch of kids like me, from all over Dallas, the fastest and strongest children from all the parks throughout the whole city.

There were dozens of

events and they gave out ribbons—blues and reds and whites for first, second, and third. I don't remember if they said "Go" or if they fired a gun or what they did, but I remember running and realizing that I was moving faster than the other kids, that I was out in front, that I was winning. I remember my blue ribbon. And I remember the exhilaration that came from knowing that I was the FASTEST! I remember it because I tap into that same feeling every time I run, every time I win.

In seventh grade, I turned out for track and I was a good runner throughout junior high, but I was never obsessed with it or as involved as some children are in sports today. I played football and ran track. My parents stressed academics, and although they didn't discourage us from playing sports, we always knew that the only way to be successful was to concentrate in the classroom.

In fact, I didn't even run track my freshman year in high school, in large part because I wanted to concentrate on my studies. It wasn't until my junior year that I realized what I could accomplish as "A Runner." And it wasn't until years later that I understood the history of running, the significance of athletes like Jesse Owens, people who came before me and who achieved more than was thought possible, remarkable people who did what had never been done. Years later, in an Atlanta hotel room with an encouraging letter from Owens's widow in my hands, it was easy to recall the first race I ever ran, a 50-yard dash through some forgotten Dallas park, the race that first introduced me to what would become my core, my dream. And it felt right that the first race I ever won was in a little Parks and Recreation meet called the Jesse Owens Games.

Waco, Texas, 1992.

TRAINING TIPS:
Turn Your Dreams
into Goals

1. DREAM SMALL.

Think like a sprinter, in small increments. If your eventual goal is the Olympics, set goals along that path—"Improve my 800 time by 1 second"; "Make the high school track team." Short-term goals are the only reliable path.

2. WRITE DOWN YOUR GOALS.

This makes it formal and gives notice to yourself and others that the work has officially begun. And it keeps your goals clear and in focus.

3. BE SPECIFIC.

If your goal is to "get in shape," you will—bad shape. It is far better to focus on specific goals, like "Run a 7-minute mile" or "Do 50 sit-ups a day." In the office, "Finish the Wilkinson report by May 1" works; "Get caught up at work" does not.

4. BE REALISTIC.

You can accomplish most things you set out to do, but it will take time. Don't shoot for something unattainable—completely outside of your nature or opportunity. At least not right away.

5. KNOW YOURSELF.

Find your *core*, that thing you are chasing. Set goals based on what you really want, not what other people expect of you. And don't assume that goals are only for the competitive areas of your life. You can make goals for family, relationships, anything.

The 200-meter medal ceremony at the 1996 Olympic Games. Frankie Fredericks (right) won the silver for Namibia, and Ato Bolden (left) won the bronze for Trinidad and Tobago.

The Drake relays, Des Moines, Iowa, 1990.

DISCIPLINE

FINITE MATH

2

Real glory springs from the silent
conquest of ourselves.

— ANONYMOUS

My form is all wrong. If you

watched the Olympics, you probably heard a track analyst say
that Michael Johnson runs too erect, too upright, and that it's
a wonder he has done so well with such unorthodox form.

It's not a wonder at all. It's hard work. Success for any of us
is a sort of mathematical formula, as complex as the varied
lives we lead. But broken down, a basic model for our lives
might look something like:

(Natural Talent + Opportunity) Hard Work = Success

It's easiest to see the formula in athletics, where commitment and preparation are often all that mark the differences
among an arena full of perfect physical specimens. Television
coverage of sports is replete with stories about athletes who
aren't as talented but who succeed on "guts" or "determination"

or whatever other word is in style to describe hard work. The same is true in other parts of our lives. To stretch an overly simple equation, if your office partner's innate abilities as a salesman (say he is naturally outgoing and persuasive) could be quantified as 10 and his work ethic (2-hour lunches, poor preparation) could be quantified as 4, then given the same opportunities, you—less talented, maybe an 8, but a harder worker, say a 6—could easily perform better. Obvious? Perhaps. But sit down and honestly evaluate yourself. Unfortunately, for most of us, there is little we can do about the first factor, natural talent. That is the only number that is fixed. But are you working as hard as you can, as efficiently as you can? Are you really searching for opportunities, trying to find them instead of just waiting for them? Honestly evaluate yourself and you might be surprised. Sometimes the most obvious is the most elusive.

As for myself, I do have natural talent, in part because of a somewhat unique body for a sprinter, a genetic mixture of my compact, muscular father and my tall, lanky mother.

But my build is my most glaring natural weakness too—shorter legs than most sprinters and that vertical form, a style that gives me power in the middle and end of a race but makes me a slower starter than many other sprinters. If I come upright too soon in a race I lose some of the driving speed that sprinters need. I came relatively late to track and field, so I have spent much of my time working on a natural style that is both my biggest strength and my biggest weakness.

Watching me run as a high school sprinter, a few coaches might've thought I'd make a pretty good college runner, but I can just about guarantee that few saw an NCAA Champion, a World Champion, or, certainly, an Olympic Gold Medalist. My own coach just hoped he'd find a leg for one of his relay teams.

The rest, I'm proud to say, has come from hard work.

I didn't even run track my freshman year in high school, as I've said. As a sophomore, I long-jumped a little and began running the sprints and relays. Honestly, I wasn't in great shape. It wasn't until my junior year that I emerged as one of the top 200-meter runners in Texas and I began to hear from a few college track coaches. The next year, my senior year, I continued to improve a little bit, and I realized that my education might be subsidized because of my ability to run.

I accepted a scholarship to Baylor University because of the coach, Clyde Hart, who had a strong reputation and who impressed me with his understanding of sprinters, his no-nonsense affection for his runners, and his interest in academics. In my first 200-meter race in college, I set the Baylor record and lost by only a tenth of a second to Floyd Heard, who was at the time the top-ranked guy in the world.

At Baylor, I competed with and against some of the best sprinters in the country, and I found out about a world of track and field I didn't know existed. I met athletes who had spent their high school careers running on national touring teams and other athletes who had moved on from college to run professionally in Europe. It was the first time I realized that there were levels of track I hadn't attained and that, incredibly, it was possible to make a good living running. It had never really occurred to me before. It was also the first time I realized what a tiny sliver of time separated me from the elite runners in the world, what a small measure of time—something like a musician's single beat—stood between me and the things I'd never allowed myself to really think about. I could suddenly see myself, in occasional

Running on the Baylor University 400-meter relay team, 1989.

daydreams, as a professional sprinter, maybe even an Olympian.

But if I were to get there, I would have to do something I'd never done before. I'd have to *really work* at track and field.

I suppose I'd worked as much as was required, but I'd never had to push myself, to attempt to do something I didn't think I could do. That's the real value of self-discipline, to be able to push yourself further than you believe you can go. We all know people who appear to do just fine on minimal effort, coasting through life, classic underachievers who ride their natural talent as far as it will take them. But upon closer look, those people are usually more harried than we ever imagine them. And when they want to go further, into that rarefied place where the truly exceptional dwell, there is nowhere to turn but to self-discipline. Even artists will tell you that creativity is nothing without hard work.

One of the qualities lacking in Americans—in all people—is self-discipline. Many of the social problems in our society are exacerbated by the expectation we have that people won't work hard, don't have to work hard, and aren't responsible for their actions. Of all the deficits in this country, the shortage of self-control and pride might be the most costly.

So what is self-discipline? It is a decision you must make that you aren't going to expect the least from yourself anymore, that you are going to commit to working harder, to practicing your skills. It is mastering the ongoing dialogue with yourself. Here's what I mean.

We all carry on a constant conversation within our own minds, encouraging sometimes (Come on, Michael, you can find that restaurant!), discouraging other times (Come on, you idiot, stop and ask for directions). Often we try to fool ourselves into doing things, or we threaten ourselves, or bully ourselves. We try to surprise ourselves, shock ourselves, insult ourselves. We reason, cajole, and finally, give up. We're like bad parents with bad kids in a crowded mall.

Anyone who has jumped off a high diving board knows those internal conversations (Come on, you wimp! Jump! Just do it! Don't think about it, just jump! One-two-three! Don't look down! Jump! All those people are staring at you! Do it! OK, go ahead and back down slowly, but grab your ankle.) There's nothing wrong with that conversation; we've all had some form of it and it can sometimes keep us from making mistakes.

More often, it is the voice that keeps us from attaining what we have decided we want. That voice can grow deafening when you're working hard, when you're in training, and when you're trying to refine your performance or achieve some goal. (Forty-nine push-ups is enough! Everyone else takes a 2-hour lunch break. What's one piece of pecan pie going to hurt?)

Self-discipline is the art of controlling that conversation, weeding out the counterproductive suggestions, asking and answering all the internal questions and doubts before you ever begin and then calmly jumping off that high diving board, doing the 50th push-up, taking a 1-hour lunch, turning down that piece of pecan pie.

It really is something like dealing with children. You need to be stern, patient, and consistent with yourself. If you fool a child into eating vegetables (brussels sprouts taste like chocolate!), it will work once, maybe twice. If you fool *yourself* into doing something, it will work once. If you bully yourself, you will naturally resent the bully—after all, who likes a bully?—and the work will be even harder. You must be honest with yourself. For me, it does no good to pretend that I'm going to like working in the weight room. It's my least favorite part of training. So I need to be stern with myself, to be patient, and most of all, to be consistent. Then when I mess up, the way a child does, I need to give myself a break, the way I would a child who has tried his hardest and still failed.

You always need to give yourself another chance. And then you have to do everything you can to make sure you don't make the same mistake twice.

I can proudly say that I've never missed a scheduled day of training in ten years. My coach, Clyde Hart, tells of the day he found me out on the track, training in a driving rainstorm, when everyone else had taken the day off. "You never know," I told him, "when you might have to run in the rain."

Coach Clyde Hart and me, June 1996.

That kind of dedication is easier to describe than it is to maintain, I know. All the inspiration in the world does little good when you're the only one in the gym, when the library is closing and you have four more hours of studying to do, when the janitors are the only other ones left in the office.

So, to make sure *I* continue working out, to make sure *you* follow through with self-discipline at school or at work, we've got to maintain the proper balance of (1) motivation and (2) habit. First, you must always remind yourself why you are doing this, what the goal is. Use anything at your disposal—

Week of May 6, 1996   weight 185
  Mon   6×200   26   1½   6×40
  Tue   2×495   50/50   7½   6×40
  Wed   starts   10 meters 5.1
          the speedmakers (3 sets) 60,70,80
  Thur 3×385   25/44   3   4×40
  Fri   starts   6×100   10.15
  Sat   3×275   29 / 28 / 27   2

Week of May 13   weight 184
  Mon   5×200   25   1½
  Tues 2×385   24/40   24/41   3
  Wed   speedmakers – 2 sets 60,60,70,70 (5) 60,70,80,90
  Thur warm up
  Fri   rest
  Sat   Atlanta 200   19.83

Week of May 20   weight 184
  Mon   6×200   26   1½
  Tue   1×495   50   10min   2×330 @ 28/40
  Wed   3×385   24/40   3
  Thur speedmakers (3 sets) 60,60,70,70
  Fri   10×100   10
  Sat   starts   3×30   40,50,60

A page from my training journal.

refrigerator magnets, a poster of your hero, a photo of yourself 20 pounds lighter, a brochure of the new car you want to buy with your raise.

Then, once again, *put it in writing.* I have a training log, a schedule of when I will run, how far I will run, when I will lift weights. If it says to run twelve 200-meter intervals with 2 minutes' rest, that is exactly what I do. I don't blur the edges of something that important. I never run eleven intervals and I never rest for 3 minutes. It is just not allowed in my house. No need for the conversation anymore, I have learned from myself—the way a child learns—that to complain will be wasted energy, that I'm not going to convince myself to shave a minute off the end or to cut the weight room for a day. A training log is the perfect tool for looking back, for looking forward, and for keeping yourself focused. It serves as both motivation *and* habit.

Now my training schedule is internalized. Each week I travel to Waco, Texas, where my college coach lives, train there for three days, and then go home and train lightly in Dallas. You might expect that I train 50 or 60 hours a week, but the truth is I usually train no more than 12 or 15 hours: 3 hours a day at Baylor and another hour or so each day in Dallas. That's it. But in 10 years, it has become so much a part of my life that the voices barely make a peep now. I hear from them in other parts of my life, certainly, but the conversations I have about training are with an obedient, happy, rewarded child. (Good workout. See you tomorrow.) That is self-discipline.

You will be amazed at how quickly self-discipline translates into something else: confidence. When you prove to yourself that you can eat a responsible diet, that you can stop smoking, that you can begin to exercise, all of a sudden heart disease doesn't seem an unbeatable foe. When you plan and follow through with your plans at work, you begin to exude a quiet sense of competence and knowing; others will see the difference in you.

For me, it is also important that when I am away from the track, I bring my self-discipline with me. If you are disciplined at home and at work, the habits are reinforced that much more. Some people like to be a different person when they're off work or away from school, but I believe that's another way of fooling yourself. I've known athletes who were different away from the sport than they were in it, and usually the strain of trying to be two people leaves both personalities burned out and exhausted. One prominent track and field athlete got too deep into the "Hollywood thing" and his performance suffered, because after a while it becomes impossible to separate your two personalities.

I have been described as confident or cocky or arrogant. I'll take the first one. My confidence is in knowing that I have probably trained harder than anyone I am going to run against. And that is because of self-discipline. If you meet me in a business setting, you will find much the same man that you would find on the track: competitive, eager to learn, and committed to doing my best.

I am also someone who can stop in midstream and reassess my training schedule. That is vital. At times, I've shifted to add more endurance work or more sprinting training, to vary the distance of the intervals I run, to spend more time in the weight room. Nothing takes more self-discipline than changing your work habits midway to your goal without second-guessing yourself. If you've succeeded in making self-discipline a habit that you no longer fight, changing those habits will be a chal-

1995 USA Track & Field
Championships,
Sacramento, California.

lenge. Approach it the same way you did initially: Adjust your training in writing, in your log; revisit your goal to remind yourself why you're doing this; master the conversation inside yourself; remain disciplined at home or in the office; and then, flat get to work.

Maybe you're figuring that it's easier for me, that I have a natural talent, that I'm genetically built to be a sprinter. In

some ways that's true, but I promise, I am not a natural at most things. I assure you there are plenty of areas where a gold medal is out of the question for me, where I have to use all my self-discipline and planning strategies just to avoid complete failure. There was, for instance, finite math.

OUT OF THE BLOCKS

Ask yourself: "Why am I doing this?"

I never liked the weight room. But it became apparent in college that to go farther as a runner I had to strap a few muscles on my lean frame. There's really only one way to do that—the weight room—and only one way to do that—self-discipline. When it comes time to practice self-discipline, don't fool yourself; go ahead and admit that fat-free cheese doesn't taste as good. It only works if the end is something you really want. Remember, this is a decision you consciously made. Remind yourself why. It's the perfect time to revisit your goals.

What lies in our power to do, it lies in our power not to do.
—**Aristotle**, *fourth-century* B.C. *Greek philosopher*

He who conquers others is strong; he who conquers himself is mighty.
—**Lao-tzu**, *sixth-century* B.C. *Chinese philosopher*

The ability to concentrate and to use your time well is everything if you want to succeed in business—or in anything else, for that matter.
—**Lee Iacocca**, *twentieth-century businessman*

Those who profess to favor freedom and yet deprecate agitation are men who want crops without plowing up the ground, they want rain without thunder and lightning.
—**Frederick Douglass**, *nineteenth-century American writer*

It is in self-limitation that a master first shows himself.
—**Johann Goethe**, *eighteenth-century German poet*

HOW FAR WILL YOU GO?

FINITE MATH

OK, I hate math. There, I've said it.

It was the only subject I really didn't like through-out all levels of school. Even so, I did well enough in math in elementary school, junior high, high school, and college, and because my other grades were good, I was a strong student, usually on the honor roll. My high school, Skyline High in Dallas, wasn't known for its athletics at all. It was a career devel-opment school, where students could get a start on the kinds of classes you usually take in college. Getting into Skyline was one of the early goals I set for myself and I approached it with the same disci-pline that I still use. I had to apply to the school,

1995 World Championships,
Göteborg, Sweden.

write an essay, and submit recommendations before I was accepted. I was very proud when I was accepted, and I was committed to doing well academically.

My goal was to be an architect, so I took 3 hours of architecture classes a day during my freshman year before realizing that I didn't really want to toil away in construction before they let me build my own buildings. I was a speed guy, and architecture was a distance runner's profession. So I switched to business, which I carried as my major into college.

"Are you going to college?" was not a proper question in the Johnson house. The correct form for that question was "WHERE are you going to college?" I chose Baylor because of the track program, but also because of its strong reputation in Texas for academic excellence.

Like most high school students, I had studied, but I had never studied the way you must in college. The first semester of college was a little bit scary, but it wasn't until the second that I was hit square in the face with the possibility of abject failure. It wasn't until I enrolled in the pit of academic despair. Finite math.

It was a requirement to get into the business school, and as such, I had to pass the course, something I'd never had to worry about before. A few weeks into the semester, I was worried.

I had done well enough in elementary school and junior high, when math classes were built around numbers. Multiplication, division, fractions, even negative numbers and simple geometry could be mastered because, at their root, they had a core set of numbers whose value we learn as first graders.

I had begun to trip up in the requisite algebra classes in high school, when *a* and *x* began to nudge their way into our equations. By the time I hit finite math, most of the numbers had been given the semester off. Finite math is arithmetic with attitude, a system of math based on statlstlcs. Basically, it is the development of a theory of the differences between successive pairs of numbers in a sequence. It is a theoretical subject that seemed to me—a very concrete kind of guy—like an indecipherable language.

I tried studying with other people. I tried studying alone. I went to the library as soon as track practice ended. I tried studying from 7 P.M. to 10 P.M. I tried studying late into the night. I almost gave up.

Finally I did something very difficult for a college student. I began going to bed at 8 P.M.

I'd always been a morning person, and I found that at 6 A.M. I had a much better chance of understanding binomial coefficients, of comprehending some monstrosity like "If Y_n is the number of ways of seating one or more persons in a row of n seats so that no two persons occupy adjacent seats, it can be shown that $Y_n = Y_{n-1} + Y_{n-2} + 1$ with $Y_1 = 1$ and $Y_2 = 2$." And so, at 8 P.M., I'd head for my dorm room—in Baylor Landing, where the track athletes lived—and I'd go to bed.

That's not to say that every night, with college life raging around me, I snuggled into bed with my calculator, dreaming of complex equations. But I set up a schedule and convinced myself that my goal (getting into the business school and eventually being successful in business) was worth doing something extraordinary. That is what self-discipline is and that is what you can do. Not many college students were going to bed at 8 P.M. at Baylor University in 1987. You owe it to yourself to find your own unorthodox way of succeeding, or sometimes, just surviving.

The perfect ending to this story would be to say that I got an A in finite math, that I set a world record for the fastest solution to a finite math equation.

Nope. I did what most of us do and I was proud of myself for doing it: I passed. Barely.

Eventually, everyone finds themselves in an area or subject, a job or a field, in which they don't have natural talent, perhaps not even the slightest interest.

And in those cases, the discipline you forge in areas where your strengths lie—the planning and goal-setting and training and constant rechecking of your on-board computer ("What can I do differently?")—will serve you better than you can know.

There are challenges we can all skate through, days when we get by because of our natural ability or the low expectations placed upon us. But you will find that self-discipline becomes especially vital at two very different and equally important points in your journey: when the goal is to finish first, and when the goal is just to finish.

TRAINING TIPS:
Crafting
Self-Discipline

1. DON'T FIGHT YOURSELF.

It's like fighting with kids: you can't win. Get the whole family—body, mind, and spirit—in on the goal. Be a good parent to yourself; be stern, patient, and honest.

2. KEEP A LOG.

Keep a record of your chase, a daily schedule of your homework or your training or your progress on a project at work—how far you've come and how far you have to go. A log provides two necessary things for self-discipline: *motivation* and *habit*. Recording your progress in writing keeps you focused.

3. DO THE 50TH PUSH-UP.

When you've committed yourself to 2 hours of homework, do 2 hours of homework, not 1 hour and 59 minutes. Six cold sales calls a day is always six, never five. The basis of self-discipline: Don't allow the edges to blur.

4. CARRY IT EVERYWHERE.

If you're trying to become more disciplined at work, add some self-discipline at home too. A clean garage might not help you get the Wilkinson account, but it will create and reinforce habits that lead to success.

5. TUNE THE ENGINE.

Don't be afraid to reassess. Is your training schedule working? Is this the path to your goals? How can you adjust?

1995 Paris Grand Prix.

1992 Olympic Games, Barcelona, Spain.

DISAPPOINTMENT

ONE MORE CHANCE

3

Our greatest glory consists not in never falling, but in rising every time we fall.

—AMERICAN PROVERB

I never go into a race

expecting to lose. It has been years since I expected anything but to win every race in which I compete. At one point I had won 21 straight 200-meter races. As I'm writing this I've won 57 straight 400-meter races, every 400 I've competed in since 1989.

Most of the time I don't even think about losing. I wrote earlier about the confidence that comes from knowing I am the best prepared, most disciplined person in the race. That translates into the belief that if I am in the race, I am going to win. After all, this is *competition*. The very point of competition is winning. Why go after something and ignore its very nature? If I'm going to run, I'm going to try to win. I'm going to do everything I can to win, and I'm going to expect to win. Every time.

And yet I know that I would not be the runner I am today if it weren't for a string of losses dating from my first years in college to my disappointing performance at the 1992

1990 Budapest Grand Prix.

Olympics in Barcelona. It was a harrowing, bitter streak that threatened to define me as someone who couldn't win the big race. But my reaction was—I think—the force that tempered my strong dedication and led directly to my performance in the 1996 Olympics. I am stronger because of those losses. Without the awful taste of Barcelona in my mouth, who can say how furiously I would have gone after both the 200 and the 400 in Atlanta?

But it is a strange balance, learning how to handle defeat without allowing yourself to think too much about it. I believe that to anticipate failure is to welcome it at some level. I've heard other sprinters say that the best they can hope to finish is third or fourth. And guess what—they usually finish third, fourth, or worse. I refuse to give myself an out like that, to give myself permission to do less than my best.

To refine my training and give myself a break before the Atlanta Olympics, I ran the 100 meters for a few months in 1994, even though I'm not as suited to run that race as I am the 200 and the 400. For the first time in a few years, I was the underdog in just about every race I ran. And yet, deep inside, I envisioned myself winning even those races. Likewise, I'm part of an ownership group that bought the Dallas Mavericks, a professional basketball team, which hasn't had a winning season since 1990. And even though I know little about basketball, I fully expect the team to win. It is the first and most basic rule: Always expect to succeed.

But, of course, I didn't win all those 100-meter races. In fact, I lost more than I won. And for all my expectations and hopes, the Mavericks still may be a big man (or two) short of being a serious contender for the NBA title.

That is the nature of the balance—the only way to deal with loss—as a horribly unwelcome guest that you know will show up eventually. And so you deny it and reject it and ignore it and laugh in its face. You toss it out into the street and push it away and fight it off, and only after it has landed square in your lap, only then do you deal with it.

When it happens—when someone else gets the promotion, when you flunk calculus, when your boyfriend breaks your heart, when you finish eighth—you handle it with grace and defiance. To the outside world, as much as humanly possible, I try to be the same person after a loss as I am after a win. Either way, I don't hide my feelings. You should be the same person when you land a huge account as you are when you can't sell dirt to worms. When you win, don't gloat. Celebrate and then move on. When you lose, cry, scream, kick, do whatever you have to do to get it out of your system. Don't mope. Mourn.

And then, while the taste is still fresh in your mouth, begin all over again the process of returning to excellence. Start by assessing what went wrong. Take the same work ethic you applied to getting here and use it to look into yourself and see why you failed. You will find two things. First, you'll find a slew of things you had no control over. It's important to acknowledge those things without turning them into excuses. One key, again, is recording. Write the reasons why you failed in two columns: one for things you can't control, the other for things you can.

The first column is very important. You must list the pitfalls matter-of-factly, without mystifying them. If a flat tire caused you to be late for a business meeting, which caused you to be nervous, which contributed to losing an account, write down the flat tire in column one. And then be done with it. Don't imagine what cosmic forces conjoined to flatten your tire at that moment. You had a flat tire. If that's where your analysis of the situation ends, you're in trouble. You have to be able to ask yourself if there were other things that contributed to what happened. You have to move on to the second column: things you *can* control.

In college, I had a devastating string of injuries that nearly drove me out of the sport. I could've moped around, wondering why some random gods of injury struck me down each year, but I decided to look a little further, to see if there was something I could do differently.

If you apply for a job and you are told, "I'm sorry, we were looking for someone with more computer experience," you can hang your head and fill out the first column: things I can't control. Or you can step back and ask yourself how you can get more computer experience. As your performance is enhanced,

1995 Prefontaine Classic, Eugene, Oregon.

you'll realize that there are really few things you *can't* control.

When you've identified the few pitfalls, the reasons for failure that you can't control, throw them away. They'll do you no good. If you bring them to the next race or the next test or the next business meeting, you'll just be giving yourself an out, an excuse for a failure you haven't even had yet.

The other column is where your work lies. It is the true measure of someone who has learned to lose. Can you acknowledge that you failed, draw your lessons from it, and use it to your advantage to make sure it never happens again? I almost never make the same mistake twice. I almost never lose two races for the same reason. After a loss, you are hungrier, angrier, and better equipped to improve your training. Most of the really great accomplishments arise out of seeming defeat.

Give yourself a quick association quiz: Think of any prominent person—athlete, actor, artist—and what are the first things that pop into your mind? The personal and professional highs and lows. We are all measured by our victories and disappointments. We are remembered by how high we climbed and how far we fell.

To assume that your life will be an uninterrupted ascension

Frankie Fredericks beat me in the 200 meters at the Bislet Games in Oslo, Norway, right before the 1996 Olympic Games.

is to fool yourself. And yet to anticipate failure is the perfect recipe for failure. That is the tenuous balance, another of those slim edges that separate success from failure. We all like to think of our lives as a succession of triumphs punctuated by occasional failures. If only that were true.

Once, when Muhammad Ali lost a title fight, a reporter asked him how it felt to lose, most likely expecting the standard athletic press conference answer.

Instead, Ali turned to face the reporter and gave him a lesson in living.

"We're all going to lose in life," he said. "You're going to lose your wife, your mother, your father. We all have losses in life, and the ones who can really over-

come those losses and just keep living . . . can come back and be successful. You can't go die because you lost. I did my best and I trained. I was in shape and I lost."

By that point in his career, Muhammad Ali had won and lost everything more times than most of us have the energy to try. He had seen the world from vantages that most of us never reach. Instead of the standard macho bluster of a professional boxing title match, Ali found and gave perspective: "We all have losses in life."

Our physical lives are not at all a string of triumphs punctuated by occasional failures, but an elusive chase—a tireless run that eventually will end in failure but that can be marked by frantic and wonderful achievements, a constant battle to take advantage of our time, to accomplish as much as we can before the end. One day I will lose more races than I can win. One day I will no longer be the fastest man on the track or, what is worse, I will no longer have the *potential* to be the fastest man. That's the day I plan to quit running, because, for me, the point has always been to go faster, to win. That's the day I'll move on to other races and other goals, perhaps, like my parents, working as hard as I can to raise a family.

Until then, I will carry the sour taste of years of defeat. Those years served me well and provided me with things I desperately needed: humility, knowledge, and a gnawing—at times, over-powering—desire to win.

1991 Mobil Grand Prix, Barcelona, Spain.

OUT OF THE BLOCKS

Ask yourself: "Is it something *I'm* doing?"

In college I was injured at the end of my first three seasons. Each time it was a legitimate injury, but instead of cursing the gods of track and moping around, I honestly asked myself: Is it me? Was I reacting to the pressure of big meets? No, my injuries were occurring before the NCAA Championships each year. Was I losing to better runners in higher competition? No, I was always ranked number one at the end of the season. Finally I hit on it. It was my training. Because of my build, I needed to work more than other athletes on strength and flexibility. Before you blame everyone else, before you quit, honestly look for ways to improve.

The line between failure and success is so fine that we scarcely know when we pass it: so fine that we are often on the line and do not know it.
—*Elbert Hubbard, twentieth-century American writer*

In the middle of difficulty lies opportunity.
—*Albert Einstein, twentieth-century German-born physicist*

He who excuses himself accuses himself.
—*William Shakespeare, sixteenth-century English playwright*

The tragedy of life is not that man loses but that he almost wins.
—*Heywood Broun, twentieth-century American writer*

LOOK INSIDE FOR THE ANSWER

GIVING IT THE ALL

The last thing I ever wanted to be was that guy who hangs around the track, or the football field, or the college, reliving his glory days. Everyone knows someone like that, the thickening ex-football player who can't seem to get on with his life, the former Big Man on Campus who is still there at 42.

I promised myself a long time ago that when I was no longer competitive—really competitive—I would walk away from track and field rather than be that guy, rather than race against other runners and my own ghost.

MICHAEL JOHNSON
62

So, in 1990, just before my senior year in college, I decided to give myself one more chance to stay healthy and then to quit running.

During my freshman year, I had broken out as a talented sprinter and, by the end of the year, had a good chance of doing well at the NCAA Championships. But I strained a hamstring in the preliminaries and that was it.

The next year, my sophomore season, at the Drake Relays in Iowa, I ran 43.4 in the anchor leg of the 4x400 relay, and one of the coaches assembling the 1988 Olympic team said that he'd take my 400 time "right now" for one of the spots on his relay team. I was excited to be running world-class times, and I could hardly believe that I actually had a shot at being on an Olympic relay team. But this time I suffered an even more serious injury at the end of the season. It was at the NCAA Championships in Eugene, Oregon, and I was leading my race, when I felt a sharp pain in my lower leg. It was a stress fracture in my left fibula. The doctors said there was a chance I could come back for the Olympic Trials, so I worked out at the swimming pool and on the bicycle and I felt my strength coming back slowly. But when the trials for the 1988 Seoul Olympics arrived, I had lost too much conditioning, and I was one of those slivers, those tiny slices of time, away from being competitive.

It was devastating to be so close, but I knew that I

still had two more years of college and a few more Olympics to shoot for. My junior year, 1989, I was back, running well and favored to win the 200 meters at the NCAA Championships in Provo, Utah. But going into the Southwest Conference Championships I strained my quadriceps muscle, and I had to miss the NCAA Championships for the third straight year.

I went to Europe to run that summer, after hearing from other runners about the incredible way that track and field is supported in France, Italy, England, Germany, Sweden, and the other European countries. Over there, sprinters, distance runners, and long-jumpers are swarmed by fans looking for autographs. We are paid like professional basketball and football players—sometimes six figures just for showing up at one meet—and we routinely compete in front of 40,000 or 50,000 people. Still disappointed from three years of coming up short, I went to Europe in the summer of 1989 hoping to be transformed again, to regain the confidence that my chase wouldn't be in vain.

I had never been out of the United States. In fact, my first airplane ride was only a couple of years past at that time. I arrived in Europe a wide-eyed 20-year-old filled with my teammates' rich stories of Paris, Berlin, and London, stories soaked in the Europeans' history, vibrant culture, and overwhelming love for the sport of track and field.

Unfortunately, my first stop was Budapest, Hungary. It was 1989, the Berlin Wall was still standing, the cold war was still relatively cold, and Budapest was a repressed, dreary place, almost Third World. Yet the meet itself was exhilarating. I didn't win, but I ran well, and the sight of professional track athletes supporting themselves the way football players and basketball players did in the United States was eye opening. I also ran in Zurich, Switzerland, and Linz, Austria, and although my performance that summer wasn't great, I could see clearly now what was possible, where my chase might lead. Of course, I was a relative nobody that summer, but other athletes were swarmed by

1993 World Championships, Stuttgart, Germany.

fans, approached by agents, followed by reporters, and wildly cheered at meets. And there was money in track and field, far more than I had ever imagined. Suddenly I could see this as a profession, not just a hobby. The sport never looked the same to me after that, and I knew that I wanted to go as far as I could, to do well in Europe, to win a World Championship, to win an Olympic Gold Medal.

I came home to Texas in the fall of 1989 and knew that I had a decision to make. The injuries that had plagued me in college weighed on my mind like an unpaid debt and I talked seriously with my coach about what I could do. That's when I came to the realization that I would leave the sport before I became THAT GUY, the one reliving his old accomplishments, with nothing else to turn to. I wanted to be successful at something, and I was willing to turn toward business or some other area to do that.

But first I wanted to give running one more chance, to make sure I had done everything I possibly could to be successful at it. I started by really analyzing the injuries. They were perplexing because I wasn't a classically accident-prone athlete, someone who pulled muscles often or strained ligaments in ordinary competition. Throughout the indoor season, I had been completely healthy and had even won a National Championship my junior year, but then, with the NCAA Outdoor Championships in sight, I had gone down again. I am not superstitious and I knew these injuries must be happening for a reason, but it was baffling.

I had always planned and set goals, but that fall, for the first time, I wrote my goal on a piece of paper and referred back to it all year. It was simple: Make it through my senior season without getting injured. If I didn't accomplish that goal, I decided, I would quit track and find something else to throw my energies into, probably business, which was my major in college.

Rather than tempting me to give up, my new goal enlivened me. I wanted desperately to find out why I was getting injured every year. My coach and I sat down and talked about my training program. We decided that my muscles just weren't strong enough, that by the end of the season, they were strained and tired.

I had already ratcheted up my training from high school. Coach Hart's fall training program at Baylor was exhausting and complete. Besides the shorter races and intervals, we ran 600s and 800s, a 1-mile time trial, and, once a week, a grueling 5 miles through Waco. Then, every Friday at 6 A.M., we met at Baylor Landing for a 3-mile run.

It was difficult to go from my high school training program (basically, none) to the regimented, full workout that Coach Hart preached. Such serious overhauls are hard to follow through with, but it was easier for me because the new workouts were still the thing I loved—running. I was still so excited to be there, to be competing.

Then, in the fall of 1990, Coach Hart and I worked up a new training schedule. This one included more of two things I'd never had the patience for—stretching and lifting weights. Coach had included weightlifting in his earlier training schedules, but I had gone about it without much energy, and in the end that seemed to be the only reason I might be pulling up lame every year.

So I went to the weight room. One day. The next day. The day after that. I did every repetition that was called for, lifted every pound on my training log, and I began to get stronger and more flexible. My own commitment inspired me. I was impressed with the progress I could make, with the dedication and self-discipline I was showing. On the days when I weakened, I reminded myself why I was there, what I was chasing. On the worst days, I returned to my goal, scratched on a piece of paper months earlier: Make it through my senior season without getting injured.

I also decided not to run 200-meter races early in the season. The explosive start of that race was hard on my body, and I ran mostly 400-meter races and relays early on, until my strength was built up. So, my first 200-meter race was in the Southwest Conference Championships. I scorched the track in 19.96, the first time I'd broken 20 seconds and just .24 seconds off the world record. The time was unofficial because it was wind-aided, but it was still inspiring to see that 19 up on the board. In the NCAAs, at Durham, North Carolina, I ran a 20.16, good enough for first place, my first-ever outdoor college championship.

It was a huge relief. I felt that all my work had paid off. For the first time, track clubs were approaching me. Agents knew my name. The European meets were beckoning. My 400 times were improving as well, and I was in the best

shape of my life. That year, at the U.S. Championships, I flew around the track in 19.90, without the help of the wind, a time within shouting distance of the world record.

1990 NCAA Championships, Provo, Utah.

At that time, no one in the world was running that fast. I had arrived. But what really pleased me was more personal than that: a message on a little piece of paper, a completed goal. I had made it through an entire season healthy.

And while we may like to imagine life as an obstacle course where we can run around all the losses, failures, defeats, and disappointments, I began to realize then that losing is an integral part of the stuff that propels us, that makes the chase worthwhile.

TRAINING TIPS:
Dealing with
Disappointment

1. DON'T PREPARE FOR FAILURE.

Trust me, when it happens you'll know what to do. If you spend time thinking about what could go wrong, it will. Fight off disappointment as if it were a pack of wild dogs. It will arrive without your help. And when it does . . .

2. LOSE WITH GRACE AND DEFIANCE.

You will be remembered by the way you win *and* by the way you lose, by your greatest achievements and your worst failures. Learn the difference between gloating and celebrating, between moping and mourning.

3. WRITE DOWN WHAT WENT WRONG.

Make two columns: things you can control and things you can't. Now take the list of things you can't control and throw it away. Don't carry those ready-made reasons for failing to the next opportunity. The other column is where your work lies. So . . .

4. GET BACK TO IT.

Don't lose the momentum of your hard training. Find some other place to channel all that energy. Set new goals. Learn. Get on with it.

5. RECOGNIZE FAILURE FOR WHAT IT IS.

Failure is a wholly necessary part of the process, the stuff of heroes and legends. Ask yourself what successful person hasn't had to rise from the bottom. Unfortunately, we haven't yet discovered an alternative route to the top.

1993 USA Track & Field Championships, Eugene, Oregon.

SLAYING THE DRAGON
73

PART II:
TRIALS

ACHIEVEMENT

AWARENESS

ANGUISH

With Coach Clyde Hart, 1996.

ACHIEVEMENT

THE GREATEST

4

It's amazing how many

people don't know how to win, how to deal with success. I'm not just talking about those people who are poor winners, who gloat or who aren't gracious in victory. I'm talking about people who work hard for their goals, achieve a few, and then are unprepared for the changing expectations, the changing relationships, the changing lifestyle, and the emotional pitfalls of their first taste of success. About people who find themselves unable to repeat their early accomplishments.

In that way, I was fortunate to have my victories paced out over several years. I know many other professional athletes— basketball and football players—and I see the pressures on a 19- or 20-year-old who becomes a millionaire before he is legally able to drink, who is promised $30 or $40 million or even more for a career that could be over when most people his age are still settling into a profession.

I graduated from college in 1990 and immediately left Texas for the lucrative European track and field season. The year before, I had run in Europe but had been an amateur. Now I was a professional, one of several hundred world-class track athletes paid a few thousand dollars each time we ran. The top athletes—Olympic Gold Medalists and World Champions—were getting closer to $20,000 or $30,000 (the real superstars a little more) per meet in Europe. People are still surprised that track and field can be such a lucrative sport. I think many Americans still think of runners as amateurs. But with million-dollar endorsements and meet fees reaching six figures, the top athletes can earn tens of millions during a successful career.

But that wasn't the case for me in 1990. I was 22 years old, six credits away from a college degree, a virtual unknown on the professional track circuit, known as much for my repeated injuries as for the NCAA title I'd won. Now I was suddenly on my own, without a team, without a full-time coach, faced with trying to support myself running.

I did.

Over the summer, I won every European race I competed in, about twenty, as I remember. After a few meets, I was being paid like the top athletes, drawing the accolades and the attention from the media and sports agents that I'd watched from the outside the year before. I had arrived.

But a few hundred thousand dollars is different from the multimillion-dollar guaranteed contracts handed out to young athletes in other sports. There was no guarantee for me. If I wanted to continue making money as an athlete, to have the

1996 U.S. Olympic Trials, Atlanta, Georgia.

good life I had imagined as a kid, I had to continue winning. If I wanted to be financially secure, I had to stick to the goals and discipline that had gotten me to that point. That was when I realized that there is much more work to be done when you've started on the curve of success and that patience and discipline are the best antidotes to the intoxication of early success. In short, take it slow.

I knew that a lucrative endorsement deal with Nike was just around the corner, but still I finished my first professional season cautiously. At the time, track athletes were first blushing with the wonder of professional pay, and all over the circuit, runners and jumpers showed me photographs of the grand new houses they'd bought. It hadn't been long since track and field athletes couldn't even think of affording a house until they retired and found "real" jobs. But after that season, I didn't run out and buy a Dallas mansion. I wouldn't have even if I could have afforded one. Instead I put my money away and returned to my little apartment in Waco, to a place where no one hounded me for autographs, to the old pickup truck my father had given me, to my cast-iron schedule of training, to the routine that had worked before.

I can't say what I'd have done if, after that first season, I'd been given a contract worth $70 or $80 million, like some young professional basketball players. But I think I would have had the same values and perspective that I have now.

Some things I wouldn't have had. First, the knowledge and experience that have come with six years of professional track and field. Second, a rich support group of friends, family, teachers, and competitors that has been built over those years.

Athletes in team sports have some advantages that I didn't. As a track and field athlete, I had to be owner, coach, trainer,

Tony Miller, a former teammate, and me, working out at Baylor University, 1996.

general manager, and performer. I had to develop a plan to handle the financial and administrative aspects of a running career as well as the competitive side. Now other runners ask my advice. And as part owner of the Dallas Mavericks basketball team, I try to counsel some of those young basketball stars about where to find the tools to deal with the problems of success. They are tips that apply to anyone.

Say you've just struck out on your own—as I did—and achieved things that others said you couldn't achieve. You lost 20 pounds. You returned for your master's degree. You earned a raise at work. And you did it all by yourself. So what's the first thing you need?

Other people. In the buzz of victory, we can forget sometimes the importance of the web of people around us: our families and friends, mentors, coaches and teachers, project teams at work and study groups at school. After college, I continued to train with Coach Hart at Baylor and to draw support from my family and from friends like Ray Crockett, a friend in high school and college who was venturing into early success himself as a defensive back in the National Football League.

There are scores of others who will be vital once you've embarked on the correct path to reaching your goals. To succeed as a well-rounded person, you will need to rely on an array of experts. If your success is accompanied by financial gain, you will need accountants and investors. I don't know what percentage of my portfolio should be stocks and what percentage bonds, so I hire an expert. If your success is techni-

With Brad Hunt and Gwen Torrence in Göteborg, Sweden.

cal, you will need technical support to continue climbing. For instance, I have a strength coach and others that I rely upon for help.

For me, the most important expert has been my agent, Brad Hunt—administrator, marketer, negotiator, and friend. When he became my agent, in 1990, Brad had already sharpened his abilities by representing other athletes, so he knew the terrain I was wandering into. But more than that, I trusted him. To allow someone close enough to be of great help, you must trust him, and that's been one of Brad's strengths.

But of all the experts you surround yourself with, the most important and the most rare is your mentor, the person whose experiences and wisdom you draw upon in your personal quest. Clyde Hart was for me the perfect guru, a plainspoken, joke-cracking track coach who knew sprinters the way no one else did. My success is in many ways a tribute to his training methods and his confidence in me. Coach Hart had set himself apart from all the other coaches during recruiting by talking about the degree I would earn at Baylor and not just the events I would run in. It was clear to me and my family that this was a man who truly cared about the athletes he coached, about our future as well as our athletic present. And now that I've had some success, he doesn't go out of his way to say "I'm Michael Johnson's coach." He is *consistent*, the same man when I win as when I lose, the same today, when I'm a World Champion, as when I was that gawky, uptight runner with potential. Along with trustworthiness, consistency is the thing to look for when you surround yourself with people who can help you on your quest. Not all of us are good judges of character, but one reliable test is to ask, "Is that person consistent?"

Some people try to find a mentor who will provide everything for them: counseling, companionship, guidance, and discipline. That is too taxing a demand for you and for your mentor. A good mentor—like Coach Hart—offers directions and driving tips from the back seat. *You* still have to drive the car. Or, as the Chinese say, "Teachers open the door, but you must enter by yourself." In the end, we all have to find our own way, to trust our own instincts. There can be companionship on the

Waco, Texas, 1991.

chase, but no one can really help you, because you are the only one who knows just what you are chasing.

In that way, your friends and family are also wildly important. They keep you tethered to the earth. They keep you humble, and yet if you're too humble they restore your confidence by giving back some of the confidence you've shared with them over the years. They help with the toughest thing you'll face once you begin succeeding: expectations.

When you were climbing, expectations came from within. Now, when you've reached your first peak, expectations will seem to come from everywhere, from your professor who wants you to get another A, from your boss who demands another project like the Wilkinson report, from your husband who hopes you will lose another 10 pounds.

The best thing you can do is to reclaim your expectations, to make sure they come from within, and to surround yourself with people who will keep you from getting too high or too low. Denver Broncos defensive back Ray Crockett has known me since high school, and he and I have been there for each other when either of us has failed. We remind each other of the hard work and dedication that got us here, and we remind each other of what we are capable of doing. We remind each other that the success we've had has come from within, not from the expectations of others.

One of the most important things I tell young athletes is to master the balance of self, to be who you are in every situation. Some people believe that they can have a public face and a private face, that they can be one person at work and another at home, that they can be ruthless in the office, for example, and not at home. Such schizophrenia is dangerous, though, and both personalities are left hurting. For athletes, this translates into what the media calls "scandals," an array of bad personal decisions: drug use, domestic violence, and other criminal activity.

I always believed that drastically changing my personal life—my personality off the track—would eventually erode my running ability. I've seen other athletes fall into a fast-paced life that they believe they control and keep out of their performance. But people cannot be carved up like that. If you are a runner, then running will spill over into every part of your life and every part of your life will spill into running. Teachers and police officers know that they cannot have two personalities. It's important to get away from your job, certainly, but you can't get away from the person, the cop or the teacher.

The test for others is a good starting place for yourself: "Am I being consistent?" "Am I being trustworthy?" And then the test continues for you, because you must ask yourself, "Am I being humble?"

It is important that you strive for humility, but not humiliation, for a cool, level-headed confidence, not a stiff, delusional arrogance. Humility for me is automatic. It is the knowledge that anyone can lose at any time. I enter every race with that knowledge; it allows me to fly and it keeps me grounded and focused on my goals.

Anyone who has had some success has heard this: "You've changed." It is one of the biggest fears for those people who are afraid to succeed, that they will leave the people they care about behind, that they will alienate the people around them: "You've changed." The best response? "Yes. I probably have." In truth, every experience changes you. After you lose 15 pounds, you may not want to drink beer and eat pizza at midnight with your dorm roommate. "You're not as much fun as you used to

Hughes Spalding Children's Hospital, Atlanta, Georgia, 1996.

be," your roommate might lament. "You're too good to hang out with the old gang." "You take yourself so seriously." "You don't drink anymore."

Of course, you have to be sensitive to the feelings of your friends. People who forget their friends when they're successful will be forgotten themselves when they fail.

However, to remain unchanged is to stand still, to abandon your chase. When you're making progress, you can't help but appear somewhat different to people on the outside. You are climbing, running, moving. Perspectives change the higher we climb, both for the person climbing and for those who choose

to remain at the bottom of the peak. There is no other way. You are going to change.

The more important question to ask yourself is "Have I changed my values?" Everything else will change. Your face will age; your waist will thicken; your personality may become brittle or soft, sentimental or hard. But your values should be constant, and unfortunately, there is no challenge to your values like success. I believe that most wealthy businesspeople are inspired by the *chase*, by the same kind of greatness that anyone else aspires to, but in a different form. However, some are sidetracked by the measurement, by the currency of business: money. It's the same with athletes sometimes, with those who measure their ability based upon their paycheck. I can think of no great thing accomplished because of greed. Money and fame work best as by-products of that hazy thing that most people truly desire—greatness. They can be pretty adornments to a worthy achievement, but by themselves, money and fame are empty and shrill rewards whose value is fleeting.

That is the ultimate test of how well you are handling success, not whether you can still drink beer with your friends until midnight, but whether your chase still runs on honorable fuel.

OUT OF THE BLOCKS

Ask yourself: "Has my motivation changed?"

When you become successful, it's too easy to confuse the trappings of success with your goals. The new house, shiny car, and fancy clothes can be inspiring, but they will only take you so far. Dig up that goal that you wrote down, reflect on its innocence, and try to see the world that way again. You can enjoy the trappings, but you can only *revel* in greatness, in the thing accomplished.

OTHER VOICES

The problems of victory are more agreeable than those of defeat, but they are no less difficult.
—*Winston Churohill, twontioth contury English statesman*

The reward of a thing well done is to have done it.
—*Ralph Waldo Emerson, nineteenth-century American essayist*

A minute's success pays the failure of years.
—*Robert Browning, nineteenth-century English poet*

Success seems to be that which forms the distinction between confidence and conceit.
—*Charles Caleb Colton, nineteenth-century English clergyman*

Experience is a dear school, but fools learn in no other.
—*Benjamin Franklin, eighteenth-century American statesman*

Only the mistakes have been mine.
—*Malcolm X, twentieth-century American civil rights activist*

TEACHER OR ROLE MODEL

THE GREATEST

When the 1990 professional season ended, I did something that apparently surprised a lot of sportswriters. I returned to Baylor to finish up those six credit hours, to take the two classes I needed to graduate with a degree in business.

I suppose the media has some expectations of young athletes, especially young black athletes, that causes them to rely on stereotypes. I can't count the number of interviews that began with the assumption that I grew up in a crack-filled ghetto, perhaps learning to run by dodging bullets on my way to school every day, that I'd risen out of poverty, ignorance, and crime to achieve greatness. Some writers seemed disappointed to have that easy, obvious story shattered, to find out that I was a serious student, raised in a

1996 U.S. Olympic Trials, Atlanta, Georgia.

solid family that wasn't well off but was well provided for, and well guided by my parents.

Those same writers made a big deal out of the fact that, faced with the opportunity to earn millions in endorsements and meet fees, I would return to get my college degree. What they didn't realize was that my desire to graduate from college was older than any track goals, that it was entirely expected in my house. Did the media laud John Kennedy Jr. for graduating from college? It's odd that something as obvious and intelligent as taking two more classes to earn your college degree is so irregular that it would be commended and used as a shining example.

For the first time, it seemed, I had ventured into that athletic no-man's-land: role model. I have to tell you, I have always been one of those athletes who cringe at those words. It's not that I object to having my behavior examined. I try to do the right thing, and I'm very good at achieving what I set out to do. But we too often settle indiscriminately on our role models and heroes. Do we really want our children to emulate a man who has shown nothing but an ability to catch a football? Or a woman with a great singing voice? Or even a great sprinter? Don't get me wrong, I'm honored that people want to run like me. I'm happy to see kids choose to wear the shoes I wear, follow my training schedule, or run the events I run. But shouldn't there be more to being a role model than that, more than taking two classes to earn a college degree?

One day recently, after what seemed like days spent signing pictures, scraps of paper, and magazine covers, I was approached by a woman in a restaurant and impatiently asked for my autograph. I asked her to wait until I was done eating. That bothered her, and later, when I did sign my name, she gently chided me for not being a better role model for her son. I considered suggesting to the woman that she didn't really know anything about me, certainly not enough to tell her son he should be like me. Surely she knew family members or ministers or teachers who would make more valuable heroes.

But it got me thinking about my own sports heroes. As a kid, I had none. My parents were my heroes; their sacrifice and discipline were the things I aspired to.

Even now, there are only two athletes who have monumentally affected the way I look at the world, only two sports heroes for me.

One is the sprinter Jesse Owens, who courageously competed in the face of Adolf Hitler's racist tyranny in the 1936 Olympics in Berlin. In the center of a regime built on the myth of Aryan supremacy, Owens—who a year earlier had set six world records in one day— shattered the myth. Treated as a second-class citizen in his own country and facing pressures that no other athlete will ever face again (Can you imagine running for an entire people, for the ideal of freedom?), Owens won four gold medals in the 1936 games. Afterward, while the other American athletes went on

Jesse Owens, 1936 Olympic Games, Berlin, Germany.

Michael Johnson, 1996 Olympic Games, Atlanta, Georgia.

a money-making barnstorming tour of Europe, Owens went home to see his wife. Because of that, he was banned from competition by petty track officials, yet he never gave up his dignity, never compromised himself.

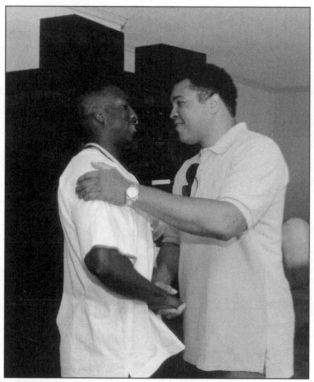

With my idol, Muhammad Ali, Atlanta, Georgia,1996.

My other hero is Muhammad Ali. In the wonderful celebrations that followed the Olympics, I met actresses and athletes, business leaders and politicians. But when I am asked about my Olympic highlight, I don't hesitate. It was meeting Muhammad Ali.

He had opened the games by carrying the torch the last leg and lighting the Olympic flame, a stirring moment for all the athletes in Atlanta. We had been teased for weeks about who might light the flame— "It's someone big," the organizers promised—but when Ali appeared, it was more fitting and dramatic than anyone could have guessed.

Later, with the games winding down, he stood across from me in an Atlanta hotel room, frozen by the Parkinson's disease caused by the damage from his boxing career. Like Jesse Owens, Ali has transcended sports. Before Ali, sportswriters, owners, and promoters created the personas of athletes, who mildly played along until they were no longer useful, until they no longer hit home runs and sold shaving cream.

Muhammad Ali changed all that. He defined himself—"I am the greatest!"—through raging success and crushing loss, refusing to allow the mythmakers to create him. His life barreled ahead, Ali always at the wheel, changing his name when he embraced the Muslim religion, protesting the Vietnam War even though it meant the loss of his heavyweight title, losing and winning back his title again and again over decades.

Ali always came back. He understood more than any athlete the inevitable cycle of things: Losing and winning are different sides of the same coin.

He rarely speaks anymore because of the disease, and when he does, it's just a whisper. Parkinson's crip-

1990 Goodwill Games, Seattle, Washington.

ples the body but leaves the mind intact, and I wondered at the frustration of that charismatic fighter staring out from a dying body. Our eyes connected, and while cameras chirped around us like crickets, he squeezed my hand and I saw the familiar determination and embrace of life in those clear eyes. And then he smiled, and just for a moment I could see right through the disease, the way he must see right through it.

I think of that moment now when I hear the words *role model*.

There are few people I respect more than Muhammad Ali and yet I could never pattern my life after his, any more than a horse could try to hunt like a tiger. Ali was brash and wildly self-promoting and his mistakes and excesses are as famous as his triumphs. I am cautious and quiet and my failings are my own. To me, the problem with role models is summed up in the old saying: "The courage of the tiger is one and of the horse another."

And yet our differences are invaluable. There is so much I can learn from someone like Muhammad Ali. I can try to avoid his mistakes, to draw lessons from his victories, and to find inspiration in the fearless way he has lived his life. Mine is a family of teachers. I believe that it is better to learn from the diverse people around us than to try in vain to emulate them, better to be a teacher than a role model.

You only get so far by mimicking someone else. In the end, being like me is a waste of time for everyone but me. And that's why I wouldn't want anyone to go to college just because I went to college. Go to college because you want to go to college, and use my experience only as an example of one way it can be done. I have become successful by looking inside myself and finding the desire and will there, by living efficiently and honestly, and by finding out who I really am. You won't find those truths inside someone else.

But if you can take some lessons from my chase, I would be honored and my journey would be more worthwhile. So I wholeheartedly offer up my story to show you where the potholes are, to share the things I've learned.

I think now about Ali and about the woman who chided me to be a better role model and I am honored that some people consider my performances on the track heroic. I certainly understand how important it is to have heroes. Standing in front of Muhammad Ali that day, I was overwhelmed by the lessons he's taught me. Before we left the hotel room, I asked for his signature and he obliged in a slow, shaking hand: *Muhammad Ali.* It is the only autograph I've ever asked for.

Four years old.

TRAINING TIPS:
Handling Success

1. DON'T SPEND IT ALL IN ONE PLACE.

The pace of success is slow, and the celebration of it should be too. Don't abandon the things that got you there.

2. SHARE IT.

Share success with friends, family, teachers, co-workers, everyone who helped you get there. Find new people to help. The minute you start believing that you accomplished something alone, you will be alone.

3. RECLAIM YOUR EXPECTATIONS.

It's nice for others to have confidence in you, but if your expecations come from the outside, you will resent them and the journey will become more difficult. The best motivation always comes from within.

4. FIGHT THE FEAR OF WINNING.

We do the strangest things to scuttle our own success. Whether it's because we're afraid of leaving our nest or afraid of falling, we can freeze when it comes time to open our wings. Be bold.

MICHAEL JOHNSON

5. FIGHT THE FEAR OF CHANGE.

Don't cling to habits, places, or people simply because they worked for you before. The only thing you can never change is your values.

1991 World Championships, Tokyo, Japan.

1995 National Championships, Sacramento, California

AWARENESS

LANE 8 5

I had become the top
sprinter in track and field, a World Champion, at 22 years old.
I was making a lot of money, walking the narrow cobblestone
streets of Brussels, Paris, and London, hounded by autograph
seekers and photographers. The 1992 Olympics were just
around the corner, and I would be the favorite to win a gold
medal in the 200 meters, which I had dominated since coming
out of college.

I was in uncharted territory, a place I had barely had enough
time to plan for, staring at goals that had arrived more quickly
than I might have imagined.

It is only after your goals and your training have been battle-
tested—after you've finished college, after you've become a
foreman, after you've broken your first 8-minute mile—that

you can accurately and honestly assess your chase so far, that you can ask yourself, "How have I done?" and "Where to now?"—questions that add up to answer the more important one—"Who am I?"

My first year.

Let's say you are climbing a mountain. When you reach the first peak, there are two things you can do. They are both vital and yet you should be careful not to spend too much time doing either one.

First, you should look backward to see how far you've come, and then you should look forward to see the next peak. That first peak is the best place to pause and look back, to see if you took the easiest route, to learn the lessons from the first climb. And it is the best place to examine the terrain ahead, to change your plans and goals, to take a deep breath and begin climbing again.

That is who you are right now—a perfect blend of your actions and your dreams, the sum of the climb you've accomplished to this point and the climbs you are still planning.

So what does it all mean? What should you measure your accomplishments and failures against?

Others, to start with. The singular uniqueness of your chase is balanced by the knowledge that others are hunting on the same mountain, perhaps for different prey, perhaps not. So who should you look to? The champions? The valedictorians? The woman who lost 125 pounds? The man who beat prostate cancer?

Of course. Their paths up the mountain may have been better than yours. And they may be ahead of you on the next trek, on the climbs you still have to make.

But you should also examine those who have taken the wrong path. I am someone who believes you learn as much from those who have failed as from those who have succeeded.

For seven years I have watched the other athletes on the track circuit to see what they do right. I have gotten advice and inspiration from many athletes, and I have tried to be quick to offer help to the athletes who seek me out.

But I have learned just as much from what athletes do wrong. I have watched prominent people in other fields and—without being judgmental—taken much from the mistakes they've made, personally and athletically.

For example, the media has made much of my relationship with Carl Lewis, one of the preeminent athletes of our time. Carl and I don't have a bad relationship; we have virtually no relationship. We've raced a half dozen times (I've won all but one), and otherwise we are cordial but certainly not friends. I have respect for Carl as an athlete; there was no better performer in big meets, in the Olympics and in World Championships. Yet I do not respect the way he's carried himself on the track circuit, the way he has responded to his own success. He has been, at various times, a bad winner, a bad loser, someone who has put self-promotion ahead of running, and someone who has imagined himself above everyone and everything around him.

Yet I learn more by watching Carl's mistakes than by watching the triumphs of most other athletes. When he unsuccessfully tried his hand at fashion designing and pop singing, I learned the value of staying within your realm. When he announced before the 1984 Olympics that he'd be bigger than Michael Jackson, I was reminded of the dangerous progression from confidence into arrogance, and I saw the way people are repulsed by unchecked ego. Even now, as he tries to be the elder statesman of track and field, Carl's grandiose personality seems to have him trying too hard to gain the things we all want: respect and admiration.

In all these years, he has failed to learn that we do respect and admire him—for the things he's accomplished in track. That should be enough.

After a graceful and stirring victory in the long jump in the

Carl Lewis and me, 1995 Prefontaine Classic, Eugene, Oregon.

Atlanta Olympics, Carl once again spoiled a warm reception by immediately campaigning for a spot on the 4×100-meter relay team, a team he'd failed to qualify for and had rejected training with. I actually thought he should be on the team since he had proved himself to be a pressure performer and we needed our best team out there. But that was the coach's decision, and it was unseemly for Carl to campaign for it blatantly. He showed a lack of restraint and humility by publicly angling to make the team and a surprising naiveté about how the public would perceive his campaign.

But that is Carl, and in the end, watching others is a spectator sport. You can only learn so much about baseball by watching a game on television. You always learn more by playing it yourself.

And you will learn much more about your own chase by looking inward.

If you've worked the way I've advised, you've written down goals ("What do I want?"), connected them with concrete plans ("How can I get there?"), and bulked them up with discipline ("Where do I start?"). You've learned from early disappointments ("What went wrong?"), recast your efforts ("What can I change?"), and found some early success.

Now it's time to really test yourself, to exceed those original goals, to realize the enormous potential that you have, to ratchet up your discipline, to work even harder. In the incremental progress of a sprinter, you've shaved a few tenths off your time, and now you have to decide if you want to go further.

You've gotten back into college; now let's see about getting A's. You've landed a new sales job; now let's see about being salesman of the month. You've opened the lines of communication with your son; now let's see about drawing him back into the family.

The first thing you will need to reach that next level, that next peak, is consistency. We've talked about consistency in your character. Consistency in your performance is equally important. You really aren't ready to move on to the next level until you can perform consistently at the high level you're at now. For example, if you want to get your weight down to 125 pounds and you're having trouble maintaining it at 135, it might be too soon to set 125 as a goal. See if you can spend a month or two at 135. And to be consistent at that weight, you will have to be consistent in your diet and in your exercise.

For me, consistency in 1992 meant eliminating the bad races and running within a few tenths of a second of my best each time I ran. It was that much more challenging because I alternated back and forth between the 200 and 400 meters, essentially trying to reach consistency in two events. It is the quality I admire most in athletes, and in everyone else, for that matter. Of course, in our quick MTV culture, consistency isn't viewed much differently from flat-out boredom, but I think it is much more than that.

Many of the qualities that we respect in other people are built on the foundation of consistency. Think about your best friends, the people you admire at work or in your family, the bands whose music you enjoy, the actors you admire, writers you respect.

Now ask yourself if they are consistent, if you know what to expect from them in any given situation. Of course, it is not their only quality, but chances are, it is the quality upon which the others are built and upon which you rely.

1992 U.S. Olympic Trials, New Orleans, Louisiana.

If you are performing and working consistently, the next place to look is at your technique, your mechanics.

In school, are you studying in the best way possible, using methods that will help you retain the information? Or are you curling up in front of the television with a textbook, talking on the telephone and painting your toenails? If your goals involve getting in shape, are you doing proper sit-ups, researching the best kind of aerobic exercise, buying the proper equipment, or are you running in jeans and clogs? If your goals involve your career, do you have the right laptop computer? Have you really researched investment opportunities?

For me, reassessment meant looking long and hard at my own technique, at my often-criticized running form. When I did have bad 200-meter races, it usually stemmed from the fact that I came out of the start too straight up. I run in a more erect position than other sprinters, and at the beginning of the race, when I should be leaning forward for a quicker, more powerful start, that can be a huge problem. I commissioned computer analyses of my running form and worked with my coach and others to isolate the muscles and training regimen that I needed to improve my start in the 200.

If you've come this far, if you've achieved some success, you owe it to yourself to reassess the way I did, to take a good look at the on-board computer we talked about earlier. I believe it's a big mistake to settle in at a certain level of performance because you will stagnate and it won't be long until even that level will be harder and harder to attain.

Next you have to examine the opportunities, the challenges you've given yourself. If you've succeeded at one task at work, it may be time to ask your supervisor for another one, to find ways to broaden and deepen your skills. After a few years, after a few successes, there is no better time to gauge the challenges you've faced. You can now run an 8-minute mile. Rather than shoot for 7 minutes, why not set your sights on a 10-kilometer race or even a marathon? Our opportunities are limited so much by the body we're born with and by our environment, it's a shame to contribute anything to those limitations. It's better to boldly defy them, to drag your short, stocky body onto the basketball court, to test your short attention span in graduate school, to challenge yourself at every turn, and to find success in places you wouldn't have dreamed of before you improved your chase with efficiency and hard work.

And that leads to the final element you need to look for inside yourself: once again, discipline. You're resting on that first peak, staring at the trails that others have carved in the hillside, assessing your consistency and your technique. Now it's time to examine your work ethic, because the mountain will get steeper; they almost always do as you get closer to the top.

I'm not specifically talking about adding more—doubling your study hours or cutting your lunch break in half. I work out now an average of 3 hours a day, 6 days a week. I could double my workout time, but it wouldn't improve my performance. In fact, it would probably be counterproductive. It's helpful to look at what other people are doing, to ask for advice from mentors and teachers. Yet I think we can all rely on our own innate sense of how much work will be required, how many hours we need to study.

What you need to do is to examine the hours you spend preparing, studying, researching, training—in general, the hours you spend practicing self-discipline and working hard toward your goals. Look for the fat on that steak. Look for areas in which you can refine and improve your workouts.

You will find something incredible when you stop to examine the path you've taken and the road ahead. You will discover reservoirs of energy and commitment that you didn't know you had, that you didn't think were possible. Sitting on that first peak, you will see trails up the mountainside that you never noticed before, you will be able to visualize the rest of the climb, and you will discover improvements in your discipline and technique to make the next segment of the trip faster. And with some luck, you might find something infinitely mysterious and wholly valuable: the ability to surprise yourself.

1996 Olympic Games, Atlanta, Georgia.

OUT OF THE BLOCKS

Ask yourself: "Is that it?"

At this point, you are working more efficiently and with more discipline than you ever have. The margin for improvement seems to shrink with every step you take. You may have gone as far with this goal as you want to go. What do you do? Quit? Only you can say. But if you've achieved all you aspire to in this field and you want to quit, you should quickly find another. And you should never give up the chase because of fear. If that is the voice telling you to quit, you owe it to yourself to keep running, to outrun the voice and conquer the fear.

Doubt whom you will, but never yourself.
—*American proverb*

Everything has its time.
—*Geoffrey Chaucer,* fourteenth-century English poet

Too low they build, who build beneath the stars.
—*Edward Young,* eighteenth-century English poet

What is strength without a double share of wisdom?
—*John Milton,* seventeenth-century English poet

WHAT I FOUND INSIDE MYSELF

LANE 8

I was going to be an Olympic Champion, that much was certain. I was in the best shape of my life, focused on a goal right in front of me, gold in the 200 meters. That spring, 1992, fresh from a World Championship in the 200, I knew I needed to find a 200-meter race in which to sharpen myself for the Olympic Trials. Before the trials, I needed to know that I could rip off a sub–20-second 200 meters.

I found a little race in Houston, where I would be the only real world-class 200-meter runner. It is much harder to run without fierce competition, so I didn't have great expectations coming into the race in Houston. At the time, only two men—myself and

1996 Olympic Trials, Atlanta, Georgia.

Mike Marsh—were running sub-20s. But in Houston, with no one to push me, I broke 20 seconds, finishing in 19.98, and I realized that I was in rare form—that perfect combination of focus and conditioning.

And then the trials arrived. Sixteen of us qualified for the 200-meter semifinals. We would be pared down to four from each race for the eight runners in the next day's finals. In the first preliminary, Marsh and Carl Lewis and some of the other athletes ran some pretty fast times, but as my group was preparing to run, a strong headwind picked up and didn't let down. A strong wind can take a half second or more off your time, and I was plainly worried as I approached the blocks. I didn't even win my heat, and our times were much slower than those in the first heat.

1992 Olympic Trials, New Orleans, Louisiana.

What that meant was that the top four times (all from the first semifinal) got to draw for the best lanes in the finals, lanes 3, 4, 5, and 6. So at the best I would draw lane 1, 2, or 7, and at the worst lane 8. I drew lane 8.

That means nothing to most people, but anyone in track knows that lane 8 is the worst lane possible. To put it in perspective, realize that no Olympic Champion or World Champion has ever come from lane 8 in a sprint. Part of that is because the better times (and therefore the better runners) usually draw inside lanes. But the other part is that lane 8 provides no room for strategy, no way to pace yourself against the other runners or to draw yourself up close to them. Because of the staggered start, in lane 8 you run the first half of the race without seeing your competitors.

I had never in my life run a race from lane 8.

The other sprinters jumped up and down and pumped their fists when the drawings were announced. They knew what it meant. I'd spent the last two years beating them in every race and they knew that lane 8 most likely meant that my quest to make the Olympics had fallen flat. Carl Lewis told reporters that I was finished.

For just a moment, I felt finished. I couldn't believe my bad luck. Had I really worked that hard, refined my performance down to the millisecond, only to be beaten by wind and a bad lane assignment? Still, I tried to push that aside and concentrate on the work in front of me. I went to bed that night and thought to myself, "These guys aren't better than I am. No matter what lane I'm in, it's still the 200 meters, and no one in the world is better than I am in the 200 meters. I can do this." I'd run 19.98 in a race where I was essentially by myself. I can, I decided, run 19.98 from lane 8.

The next day, I walked out on the track and went through my warm-ups. But this time, my focus and intensity were different. I looked behind me and saw all the other athletes staggered around the edge where we were to start, guys I'd spent my career chasing and catching, reeling them in and leaving them behind as I tore to the finish.

Today they would be chasing me. It's a profound difference. I let my eyes move from one to the next and, for that moment, I hated every one of them. I hated them for celebrating my misfortune, but mostly I just hated them because I was about to compete against them and they were doing everything they could to make sure I didn't succeed. I hated them because it was me they were chasing.

From the sidelines, my coach said he'd never seen my face that set, my eyes so focused. I glowered from under a tense brow at every other runner on the track that day, stared them down and sized them up. I was in something my coach and I would later call the zone—the Danger Zone—because that day everyone on the track was in my sights, in my zone, in imminent danger. Other athletes have talked about my focus on the track. They say they've learned not to pat me on the back or try to make small talk on the track because they know I'm somewhere else. That day, I found a place to go where I felt the power of competition and the singular strength of my own commitment.

To this day, it is the most outstanding example of focus and determination that I can remember, and it

is the model for the mental state I try to use now when I run.

I was ready to run, not ready to get it over with but ready to compete, to move, to fly. The gun went off and I was launched out of my blocks, hurled out into my lane. The 200 meters is all fury. Chased by seven other people striving for the same thing, I ran away from them all, won the race, and finished in 19.79 seconds, just seven hundredths off the world record, the best time in the world in four years. I was going to the Olympics as the top 200-meter runner from the United States.

When the race ended, so did the fury of the Danger Zone, and I celebrated with some of the other runners and took a deep breath. I'd learned more about myself that day than I figured I could. I'd found a deep store of power and aggression and raw competitiveness and I'd ridden it to a victory that no one else expected. That is the joy and the secret of athletics, and I was thrilled to find in myself veins of it even richer than I'd ever imagined.

Barcelona, Spain, 1991.

TRAINING TIPS:
Toward Awareness

1. TAKE STOCK.

Don't get so caught up in your chase that you get off
the track. Take a little time and revisit your goals, look
back at how far you've come, pat yourself on the back a
little. Then look forward to where you are going.

2. LOOK AROUND.

Study the people who are attempting things similar to
you. Is there something successful that other people are
doing that you aren't? You can also learn just as much
from those close to you who are failing.

3. STRIVE FOR CONSISTENCY.

You are in this for the long haul. Try to reach a level of
performance at which you always know what to expect
from yourself. Be consistent throughout your life.
Steadiness may not be glamorous, but it works.

4. CHALLENGE YOURSELF.

This is the flip side of consistency. New challenges keep
you from burning out and becoming bored. And they can
reveal new paths to your dragon.

5. MATCH YOUR DISCIPLINE WITH EFFICIENCY.

Working harder is not always the answer. But working better almost always is. At this level, small improvements in your effort and your effectiveness will pay great dividends.

ANGUISH

BARCELONA 6

> Man is not made for defeat. A man
> can be destroyed, but not defeated.
>
> —ERNEST HEMINGWAY

I was sharp. I was fit, focused,
and hungry.

I was ready. I had missed my opportunity in 1988, but as the 1992 Barcelona Olympics approached I was in the best shape of my life, mentally and physically. I'd never been so prepared, so close to my goals.

I'd won the 200 meters at the World Championships in Tokyo in 1991 and then, incredibly, I'd come back from lane 8 to win the 200-meter Olympic Trials with my best time ever, a close shave from the world record. I'd also continued to win every 400-meter race I entered and, a month before the games, ripped off a sub–44-second 400, my first ever.

Earlier, I had considered trying to win both the 200 and the 400 in the games, something no one had ever accomplished in a major meet, let alone in the Olympics.

Besides the emotional and physical transformation that would be required (something like switching from figure skating to ice hockey), running both races would mean running preliminary heats of both on successive days or, quite possibly, on the same day. In the end it was very likely that I would just lose both races from fatigue or from the competitive confusion of switching back and forth.

The racing schedule wasn't set up for it, and I couldn't very well ask the Olympic committee to rearrange the schedule since I'd never even run both events in a meet. I did, however, want to run the 4×400-meter relay, which was more feasible for me.

So after the trials, I revisited my goal sheet and my plan—my training schedule. Everything looked to be in place then. I was in top shape, training well, just a month or so away from my first individual and first team gold medals. Everything that I could control was going according to plan.

Of course, when you are poised on the verge of a major success like that, you have the most at stake. But I wasn't nervous. As I've said, the kind of confidence drawn from macho posturing or blind vanity ends up being hollow and ineffective. The only confidence that works is the kind drawn from the knowledge that you are working harder than anyone else, that you are in better shape, that you have tighter focus and an unflinching will. That's exactly where I was in the weeks leading up to Barcelona. What was there to be afraid of? What could happen?

Earlier, I talked about losing—about the tight balance between not preparing for it and handling it well when it finally arrives. But when you begin performing at top levels in your field, there is another kind of loss you have to be aware of, and for this one, there is no balance, only raw disappointment. It's the kind of loss that causes you to limit yourself and sometimes ends your chase completely. It's the kind of disappointment that can make people give up—complete, catastrophic failure.

It's freezing during the biggest sales pitch of your life or flunking your law school finals. It's binging and gaining back the 35 pounds you lost and another 15 a week before your high school reunion. It's blowing the free throw in the championship basketball game.

Or losing in the Olympics.

However, the goal is not to prepare for catastrophic loss or even to learn how to deal with such total failure, although it may become necessary for you to learn how to get over it. No, the most important thing to get over is the *fear* of catastrophic loss.

The fear of complete and total failure is what keeps many people from attempting anything truly outstanding. These are classic nightmares: opening your briefcase during the big meeting and finding nothing but blank sheets of paper; standing at the free-throw line and seeing the basket a mile away; going on a date and making a complete idiot of yourself.

Usually when we imagine failure, we don't imagine the everyday, mundane failure, the common mistakes and shortcomings that are the true face of loss. We don't usually imagine losing as just a shiver away from winning, an incremental shortcoming of training, logistics, or focus—even though that's what most failures look like.

Instead, we imagine falling flat on our face in front of everyone we know and having the world mock us. Think about it. When you imagine asking a girl out, you don't think she'll say, "Maybe" or "This weekend's not good for me, how about some other time?" You imagine a complete lapse of your communication skills and the girl laughing in your face.

When people say they are afraid to fail, that's often what they mean: They are wildly, irrationally afraid of catastrophic failure.

To overcome it, you must do in theory what I did in life, look catastrophic failure right in the eye during the biggest test of your life. Only when you've done that; only when you've demystified it; only when you've looked at all it has to offer and said, "I can handle that"; only when you've put it in perspective; only then can you think about moving on.

The first thing you need to do is to imagine your worst fear, to let your mind race off in the direction of nightmares. But don't allow your mind to be general; imagine specifically what might go wrong. Fear of failure is a thing we drag with us from our childhood. It is a big scary monster that hides behind trees; you have to call it out into the light by imagining the failure in grim, perfect detail.

Then it's important to separate the possible from the impossible. Realize that in the history of American business, no sales meeting has ever gone as badly as the one you imagine; or understand that coaches don't usually make cuts in front of the whole school. Force your recurring nightmare to be realistic, and then you can see that the results of failure aren't as bad as you imagine. If your sales pitch fails, what's the worst that can happen? If you don't make the cheerleading squad, then what?

Our nightmares of complete loss usually include an audience, failure in front of people we know and want to impress. But in truth, when you lose, you lose of your own accord. So in the end, the expectations of outside people cannot touch you. You're above that when you're working hard, when you're working for yourself. Those other people weren't there with you in the weight room, or in the library studying, or in the office working late. The idea is simple: If they don't do the work, they don't get the reward of expectations. Only you are allowed that luxury. Take away the expectations of others and failure is a lot less scary.

There are two other things to do: First, realize that you can handle any loss. If you've used goals and plans, discipline and realism, then you will find that handling loss is one of your strengths, an untapped side effect of the self-control and emotional maturity that you're gaining. You can handle adversity because that has been a part of your everyday training. You have met and missed goals, but you have realized that the one constant, the thing you fall back on, is the chase itself, the cycle of setting goals, making plans, and taking your best run at what you want. You'll find that you knew going in that losing was part of that cycle. Even losing in the biggest test of your life. Once you've demystified the catastrophic failure, you see that it is like any loss—and as humans we all know innately how to lose.

With my parents in Atlanta, Georgia, 1996.

The second thing to do is to keep it in perspective. (It's not the end of the world.) I'm sure you have your own way of putting things in perspective, of realizing that your problems pale in comparison with those of the millions of people in the world who do not have enough to eat or the people you might even know whose daily battle isn't to become an executive or to get an A in Spanish, but simply to survive.

Again, there is a balance you want to achieve. Don't minimize what you tried to do. Don't minimize your training or your commitment. Putting deep failure in perspective is not saying to yourself, "Oh, that wasn't important anyway." If you do that, you will unconsciously say that the next time you are tested, and you will believe it. The truth is, your chase is very important to you. Putting failure in perspective is simply saying, "I can handle that. I can keep going."

Be realistic about your abilities and your preparation; acknowledge that you've worked hard and are in a good position to succeed. Finally, imagine yourself succeeding in the same concrete way that you imagined failure, not in a wild pipe dream, but as realistically as you can. Visualize what it will look and feel like to win. Get the taste of loss out of your mouth. Replace it with what you want to happen, what you expect to happen, not what you hope *doesn't happen*.

In the end, conquering the fear of abject failure is simply an act of realism strained through confidence. You know that it could happen, but you have to realize that it won't be as bad as you think, that the world won't end, and that if you are prepared, you are much more likely to succeed.

That said, of course, it may happen to you. In any race, seven runners will not win. So there is a good chance that you will lose in the biggest meet of your life, blow the biggest job interview of your career, miss a free throw with the game on the line. And for that, the only solace I can offer is time. You will need time and you will get time. You must use it to renew, refocus, retrain. Pain and sorrow fade, and the feelings you are left with can become great motivators.

My biggest loss was essentially behind me in a few weeks, but I carried its taste with me for four years. It was the taste of a plate of sausages and other meats, a mixed grill sampler at an out-of-the-way Spanish restaurant where meats and peppers hung enticingly in the windows. My failure began with a good friend, a nice ambience, and a tasty, carefree meal.

OUT OF THE BLOCKS

Practice compassion.

In my races, one person wins, seven others don't. It's something I can never overlook. There are students flunking in desks near yours, sales representatives missing their quotas in offices next door. It seems easy to blame those people for their own failures, but think back to your own mistakes and misjudgments. No one sets out to flunk, to fail, to fall on his or her face. Your own failures will be more bearable when you've looked at others with real empathy.

OTHER VOICES

The harder you work, the harder it is to surrender.
—*Vince Lombardi, twentieth-century American football coach*

When you believe in things that you don't understand then you suffer.
—*Stevie Wonder, twentieth-century American singer*

There are defeats more triumphant than victories.
—*Michel Montaigne, sixteenth-century French essayist*

I say to you today, my friends, that in spite of the difficulties and frustrations of the moment, I still have a dream.
—*Dr. Martin Luther King Jr., twentieth-century American civil rights leader*

LOSING THE BIG ONE

BARCELONA

The next morning my agent, Brad, still looked sort of green. "I was so sick last night," he said. He'd gotten up about 2 A.M. and had spent the rest of the night in and out of the bathroom. He thought he might have gotten a mild case of food poisoning.

For two straight nights in the summer of 1992, Brad and I had gone to a restaurant called El Candil, a popular little restaurant on a cobblestone street in Salamanca, Spain. We were in Salamanca for one of the last meets before the Barcelona games, one last tune-up to make sure I was ready. I was. Three days after winning a 400-meter race in London, I'd won the 200 meters in Salamanca in just under 20 seconds, right where I wanted to be a few weeks before the Olympics. After the meet, we'd gone back to El Candil for one last dinner before heading out the next morning for the United States. Brad thought maybe that's where he'd gotten sick. But I had eaten the same thing as Brad—the mixed grill sampler—and I felt OK. I was a little tired and weak, like I had a hangover, but certainly not like someone who had food poisoning.

That day, with Brad still trying to settle his stomach, we drove to the airport in Madrid to fly back to the United States. I slept the whole way to Madrid, and when I awoke I felt a little queasy and incredibly thirsty. I was going home to Dallas for one last bit of training, to fine-tune the machine. But during the flight, I couldn't even stay awake. I slept the entire 12 hours. I'd slept most of the last 24 hours and I still felt fatigued and nauseated.

My brother picked me up at the airport and took me to my house, where I just collapsed again, right back asleep. For days I alternated between a bubbling sick stomach and a thick, overpowering fatigue. And then I would feel better for a day and the following day be sick again. I tried staying with my parents, on the bad days, and I still couldn't muster the energy to eat, let alone train.

1992 Olympic Games, Barcelona, Spain.

Days stretched into a week and then two. When I finally made it to a scale, I'd lost 10 pounds.

I began to feel better in the days before I was to leave for Barcelona and gained back some of the weight. I worked out as well as I could, and it seemed as if some of my strength was returning. I felt confident enough when I arrived in Barcelona. I'd dominated the 200 meters for a couple of years now. There was no reason why I couldn't bounce back in time to win a gold medal.

When you make the Olympic team, you are happy, of course, but it doesn't hit you right away. I didn't fully appreciate making the American team until the opening ceremony in Barcelona. We marched through that packed stadium, the flashbulbs like a hailstorm around us, behind the American flag, and I had a new perspective. Usually my motivation is the competition itself, running to represent myself, to win for the drive inside. But now I was running for my country. It's something we may smirk at now, serving our country, as if all the work that needed to be done was completed by our ancestors. I know that running a race pales in comparison with giving your life or serving in the armed forces, but it was thrilling for me to feel a motivation so deep and profound as the honor of representing my country.

Yet the race itself would be on my shoulders alone. As the preliminary heats of the 200 meters approached, I was as confident as before any other race. With the European odds makers listing me as a heavy favorite and the media speculating on whether I could break the world record, I thought back to the trials, to the race I had run from lane 8.

My plan in the first round was to run really hard on the first curve and then shut it down—coast the rest of the way—in the place where I usually had the race wrapped up, to conserve some energy for later races. I burst out of the blocks and ran the first curve and I realized that there was someone running with me. That hadn't happened in quite a while. He was right there and I couldn't shake him, no matter what I did. Running full out, I barely won my heat, and I began to wonder what was going on.

I tried to tell myself that the race had been so close because I had been out of competition for so long, but in the quarter-finals, it was more of the same. In that race I finished second, running all out. The second burst that I had planned to save for the finals just wasn't there. I knew now that something was very wrong, that I had misjudged how seriously ill I had been in the weeks before the Olympics. I had gone from favorite to barely world class.

We lined up for the semifinals in the thick, electric air of Barcelona and I stepped into my lane and tried to find the zone where I tap into my concentration and determination. I had to convince myself that I could still win. Otherwise why even run? My rational mind was telling me that at best I had a fifty-fifty chance of finishing in the top four and making the finals. Yet at the same time I told myself that I had beaten every one of the men I was running against, that I was the same runner I'd always been, that I could dip again into the reserves of power that had carried me this far.

As I bowed into the blocks, every muscle strained and I set my mind to work on details: the three zones of the race and my plans for the next 20 seconds. For just a moment everything was OK, and I might have been alone on the track, competing only against myself, against my expectations and the success of my last few seasons. But the gun cracked, and in the 2 hundredths of a second it took us to respond, like geese startled from a pond, the other runners squeezed out ahead of me and I was chasing desperately, not running away from the others but struggling to catch them.

It had been so long since I'd seen a race from the middle of the pack—the release of runners ahead of me, the backs of spikes and the lean at the finish line.

I finished SIXTH. The top 200-meter runner in the world for 3 straight years, the prohibitive favorite to win a gold medal, and I hadn't even qualified for the finals in the Olympics. I slumped to one knee and just stared at the ground, suddenly an afterthought in these games. I was exhausted. Devastated.

Another American, Mike Marsh, won the gold with a time of 20.01. I was glad for him, but it was hard to watch someone win the gold running almost a quarter-second slower than I'd been running just a few weeks before the Olympics, before my food poisoning.

I went back to the hotel room and just sat there. I didn't cry or throw anything; I just sort of shut down. I wanted to skip the 4x400-meter relay because I couldn't imagine competing below my peak. I couldn't picture going out there and not believing that I was the fastest man on the track. But Coach Hart and my family convinced me that I should run, so I did, turning in the slowest leg on our team but helping us win a team gold medal. On the medal stand, I wondered if I would be one of those athletes who is at the top of his sport but never wins the biggest event—like a talented boxer who blows his only title shot or a great baseball player who never makes it to the World Series.

But when I left Barcelona, I decided to leave my negative thoughts there too. Whatever feelings I brought back to Dallas about the Olympics, self-pity

and bitterness would not be among them. I knew I would feel bad. I'm not someone who can hide his feelings, or who even tries to. But I would not sit around moaning "Why did it have to happen to me?" when I knew perfectly well that it happened to me because it happened to me; that there was a possibility of it happening all along; that there is always a possibility of it happening.

I didn't leave my apartment very much. For the first few days, I didn't watch TV, didn't listen to music. I just lay there, resting. After a while, I hung out with my friends, went out, listened to music, and healed the way someone would after any crash. I didn't avoid my friends and family, and I tried to accept their best wishes as gracefully as I'd accepted their congratulations when I was on top. I did what we should all do after a deep failure. I mourned a little and then I moved on.

After a couple of weeks, everything seemed to slide into perspective the way your eyes adjust to changes in focus. I would have to wait four long years to try for another Olympic Gold Medal, and there were no guarantees that I would be in my best physical shape. Yet there were many other races between now and then. Maybe they lacked the prestige and visibility of the Olympics, but they still offered that 10-year-old's exhilaration—the intertwining thrills of competition and speed.

I had lost the biggest race of my life. And yet the

sun rose the next day. And the day after that. My usual track off-season was just beginning, so I decided to take some time off to reflect, to begin the painstaking task of drawing up new goals and plans, to begin hunting the other dragons out there.

TRAINING TIPS:
Fear of Failure

1. IMAGINE IT.

I know, I told you not to prepare for defeat, but this is different. You can't conquer this fear until you recognize it. Catastrophic failure is scary as long as it's a shapeless thing off in the distance. Demystify it by getting a good look at it.

2. MAKE THE EXPECTATIONS YOURS.

Too often, the thing you are really afraid of is failing to live up to other people's expectations. In truth, most people are too involved in their own chase to think too much about yours. Yours are the only important expectations.

3. GO BACK TO OLD FRIENDS.

Fear of failure is best fought with *confidence*, *realism,* and *discipline*—the qualities you've used to get this far. Be confident that you are ready, realistic about your chances, and disciplined in your work habits. It's all you can do.

4. NOW IMAGINE WINNING.

In detailed, matter-of-fact thinking, go through the steps you need to succeed. Get the taste of loss out of your mouth and put your concentration where it can be useful: on the task ahead.

5. USE YOUR FAILURE.

If you do fail, don't be afraid to draw on it for inspiration. In a way, it is a great gift. Failure deepens us, puts nice lines in our faces, gives us great wisdom.

Barcelona, Spain, 1991.

PART III:
THE GAMES

PERSEVERANCE

PRESSURE

PERFORMANCE

Anchoring the 4x400-meter relay, 1995 World Championships, Göteborg, Sweden.

PERSEVERANCE

DREAMING
THE DOUBLE

7

When hungry, eat your rice; when tired, close your eyes. Fools may laugh at me, but wise men will know what I mean.

—LIN-CHI

I was 24 years old and I was

ready for a break.

For six years I had devoted my life to track and field, trained relentlessly most of the year, lived between Dallas and Waco, spent the summers running in packed stadiums in places I'd never even considered as a kid. It was (and is) a tiring, hectic way to live, carrying your life around in a couple of suitcases, eating hotel food and going for walks on narrow foreign streets.

I think that during those years, as now, I maintained my balance and kept the other sides of my life as full as my competitive side. When I finished working out, that was the end of it for the day. I didn't look back. To me, it's just another part of discipline: making sure that you don't do something that will either interfere with achieving your goal or interfere with your happiness. Remember, that's the reason you set out after this dragon—to make yourself happy. So I dated and I hung with my friends and always made sure that I had a rich life outside the track. Still, in the wake of Barcelona, I felt the need to slow down and relax a little more than usual.

Waco, Texas, 1992.

It is important that in the middle of your chase you take time to look around at the rest of your life, take stock, make sure you aren't ignoring your family or your friends or yourself because of your devotion to your goals. Being successful will be empty if you arrive there alone, and your success will be short-lived if you haven't managed to keep your balance.

To keep going, to really persevere after years of effort, success, and failure, you may need to recapture your perspective. No matter what the profession, there are people who burn out because they become consumed by their careers. This is one of the times when you need to trust your on-board computer. Your body will tell you when you need an extra hour of sleep; your mind will tell you when you're in need of companionship. Listen. This is something only you can tell yourself. How much time off do you need? Where do you need to recharge?

For the most part, the fall of 1992 was a normal off-season for me, a couple of months spent hanging out with my family and friends, seeing movies, going fishing, letting the motor slow down a little bit. I didn't dwell on what had happened in Barcelona. I didn't sit around feeling bad. I bought a house.

After three lucrative years as a professional runner, I'd saved up quite a bit of money and I could afford the kind of home I had always wanted. House hunting was a pleasant distraction after Barcelona, and I found a nice suburban four bedroom house on the shore of Lake Ray Hubbard, near Dallas, a quiet place where I could think and get out on my jet ski for a little well-needed speed.

Perspective isn't something you consciously chase. Often you find it in places that are as far from your chase as you can possibly get. Perspective is in the quiet of a walk, the wisdom of a good book, or the harmony of your favorite music. I find it sometimes in the slow peace of fishing.

I probably only go fishing seven or eight times a year but it's very necessary time for me. Few things could be more different from my nature. I am into speed. There is nothing slower than fishing. I am an organized, impatient person who likes to know the result before I begin. Fishing requires more patience than organization, and you never know when you might get skunked or when the catfish and bass might leap up onto shore and demand to be cleaned and pan-fried in onions and butter.

There is no better way to put your life in perspective than to drop a line into a still lake and to watch the world around you.

You can't use goal-setting to put your life in perspective; there is nothing tangible to accomplish. Perspective isn't something you work at gaining. Don't go to the lake with a checklist of things to do. You don't have to have deep thoughts or come to any conclusions. You don't have to put together a pro or con list or write down the way you plan to regain perspective. It's something that will just come. When you've really seen the lake and the shore and the hills beyond, when you've caught enough fish, when you've gotten away from the things that usually haunt you, then you will have accomplished it.

For me, the 1992 off-season was only a little bit longer than any other and didn't feel much different. I set back to work in the fall the way I always do, driving down to Waco to train with Coach Hart and the Baylor track team. The last stings of Barcelona faded with the familiar pattern of intervals, endless 200s in the windy heat of Waco, 350s and 400s, 450s and 600s, with the rest time between races figured to the second, days spent in the weight room or perfecting the technical bits of racing—the start, the corner, the burst, the overwhelmingly familiar comfort of the track.

You realize, after a while, that the work itself is a big part of the chase, completely necessary all by itself.

I went back to my other routines as well. I wrote down my goals for that year, all leading up to the 1993 World

1993 World Championships, Stuttgart, Germany.

Championships in Stuttgart, Germany, where I planned to go after the 400-meter title. World Championships are held every two years, and since I'd won the 200-meter title in 1991, I wanted a 400-meter championship to go with it.

So I concentrated on the 400 that year, finished the professional season in Europe ranked number one, and then won the 400-meter World Championship.

I'd won just about every race I ran in Europe, and my life changed dramatically when I flew there every year. I could walk unnoticed down any street in the United States (except maybe in Dallas), but in Europe I was recognized everywhere and—like other elite runners—treated something like a rock star.

In some ways I'd accomplished just about everything in Europe that I set out to do. But I still had unfinished business in America. The Olympics. As the 1993 season ended, I was already thinking about the 1996 games in Atlanta.

Yet I knew it was too early to set those goals. A sprinter's life is incremental, one burst, one race, one season at a time. Of course Atlanta was already in my thoughts, but I needed to find other challenges in the meantime to keep myself sharp. Focusing on a goal three years in the future would just about guarantee that I arrived there with an empty tank. I was also worried about burning out before 1996, about burying myself so deeply in preparations for the 200 meters that I no longer got the thrill from racing—that 10-year-old's excitement—that was one of the things that powered me.

That's a question you will ask yourself at some point, whether it's when you're facing graduate school after four years of college or when you're starting your tenth year at the company or when you've gone five years without smoking. How do I keep going? How do I keep my skills sharp, my work habits strong, and my motivation pure? How do I persevere?

The first key is that old friend consistency. We talked about its importance in your character and in your performance, but it's also one of the keys to long-term success, to persevering. After a period of time, you may try to rest most of the time and only call up your best performance during the big game. You may save your best study habits for finals week or coast at work until the end of the sales quarter. That will work once, or twice, but one time you will wait for the big game and your top performance will not come. It's a muscle that weakens when you don't use it.

Another tip: Simplify. We allow our lives to get so complicated sometimes, so twisted around our dreams and wishes, that they can be choked off by the stress and the difficulties we create for ourselves. In 1994, when I had so many other things going, I moved out of the house I'd bought less than two years earlier. Your life is a thick steak with a little bit of fat that can always be trimmed. For me, mowing that lawn and taking care

Waco, Texas, 1991.

of that house was excess fat, slowing me down. There will be other lawns to mow, I told myself. Now, I needed to make my life as simple as possible.

The other key for me was to find new challenges, to give myself a short break from my primary goal, without—and this is vital—losing my focus and discipline. So, in the 1994 season, I ran the 100 meters for a few meets, just to see how well I would do. I only won one of the handful of races I ran, but it was a nice break and it kept me in top shape and in competitive spirit. Toward the middle of the season, I realized that I was ready to get back to my specialty. The Goodwill Games were coming up and I wanted to run the 200 meters again.

I only had two weeks. It would be a severe test of my focus. I returned to Waco and trained every day. I only ran one race before the Goodwill Games in St. Petersburg, Russia, but went to the Goodwill Games and won the 200 meters. It was a good reflection of my training and my ability to concentrate. It was also rewarding to win again in international competition.

And it was fun. In the end, that's the best way to persevere: Remind yourself of the reason you started on this course in the first place. My best motivation has always come from the pure joy of running and competing, from the same thrill I got running as a 10-year-old. Have you ever known a 10-year-old to burn out? Find your initial motivation, the reason you became an architect. That's the secret to persevering. And persevering is the secret to the really great accomplishments—the kind that I began to talk about out loud in late 1994, when I began thinking about Atlanta again, when I began wondering if I could do something that had never been done before.

OUT OF THE BLOCKS

Go fishing.

Or jogging. Or to the library. Or whatever. Just get out and do something different. There is a point in your studying or working or training when the work you're putting in becomes counterproductive, when you stare so long at something that you lose focus. The best cure can be to get away from it, to go fishing or to do whatever relaxes you, whatever will get your mind off the Wilkinson report or away from microbiology. And don't feel guilty about it. What you are doing is more valuable than you might ever know.

OTHER VOICES

A simple song might make it better for a little while.
—*Sly Stone*, *twentieth-century American singer*

The real and lasting victories are those of peace and not of war.
—*John Milton*, *seventeenth-century English poet*

Yo, but I ain't trippin', I'm just kickin' it.
—*Dr. Dre*, *twentieth-century American rapper*

Our life is frittered away by details. . . . Simplify. Simplify.
—*Henry David Thoreau*, *nineteenth-century American writer*

Let us strive on to finish the work we are in . . .
—*Abraham Lincoln*, *sixteenth president of the United States*

Now the trumpet summons us again . . .
—*John F. Kennedy*, *thirty-fifth president of the United States*

PERSEVERING

DREAMING THE DOUBLE

Of course, it had always been in the back of my mind. Why wouldn't it be? I had been the top-ranked 1990, '91, and '94 runner in 200- and 400-meter and number one in the 400 in 1993. I had been a 200-meter runner a lot longer than I'd been a 400-meter runner, so I guess that was how I saw myself. But now I felt mature enough and in strong enough shape to try for gold medals in both races.

No one had won both races in a major meet since a guy named Maxey Long, before the turn of the century. In the 1960s, the great sprinter Tommie Smith was consistently among the best in both events, but even he never won both events in the same meet. The conventional wisdom was that it was just too tough a transition, that you couldn't switch from the

1995 World
Championships,
Göteborg, Sweden.

raw power of the 200 to the patient strategy of the 400 without losing your edge in both races.

That hadn't stopped me from thinking about it. First, in 1991, I talked with my coach about the possibility of running both races in Barcelona. He agreed that it would be great, but there was obviously no way the schedule would accommodate it. More important, we agreed, was winning an individual gold medal in Barcelona. Even after the disaster of Barcelona, the double remained in the back of my mind.

As the 1995 season opened, I knew that I would have to decide soon so that I could begin lobbying the International Amateur Athletic Federation (IAAF) to change the schedule of the races. I talked to my family and my coach and my friends, but the decision was always going to be mine. There was the possibility of another failure in Atlanta and the thought that maybe I should just concentrate on one race, win my individual gold medal, and let it go at that rather than push my luck. But when I thought back to Barcelona, it was clear to me that my failure was due to the food poisoning. I'd gone out the next couple of years and won everything in sight. Barcelona was a fluke.

And I had such a rare opportunity in Atlanta. How many of us get to do something that's never been done before? I didn't want to endanger getting at least one gold medal, so I hinged my decision on the

Olympic schedule makers. They were getting started, so we contacted them and asked them to change the schedule so that I could attempt to win both races. I didn't need much, an hour or two, just enough separation so the finals of the 400 didn't overlap with the early rounds of the 200. I thought they might accommodate me, but if they didn't I wasn't going to torture myself by running both races.

The IAAF said no.

I have described myself as a realist, and for a realist that no should have been the end of it. But for once I listened more to my intuition than to my careful scrutiny of the situation. Somehow I thought that if I could go out and win both races somewhere, the IAAF would have to see that I was serious and change the schedule. There was no proof of that, no indication from the committee that its decision was anything but final. Yet I had a hunch. And hunches are something that don't usually get very far with me.

In 1995, the U.S. championships were held in Sacramento. It would have been easier to attempt the double at a professional meet in Europe, where there are no preliminary heats, just one 200-meter race and one 400. But I wanted to win in the Olympic format, with several rounds compressed into a short amount of time. And to get to the World Championships, I'd have to qualify first in the U.S. Championships.

There was a lot of attention focused on what I was

attempting in Sacramento, but for the most part it was just a competitive oddity, something that would gain significance as the Olympics approached. Certainly my competitors didn't say anything to me about it, although I'm sure a few hoped that running both races would fatigue me.

With Jeff Williams at the 1995 World Championshiips, Göteborg, Sweden.

It didn't. When it came down to the races them-selves, I didn't do anything differently. For the last six years, I'd been a 400-meter runner one week, a 200-meter runner the next. Now the transition was down to nothing. In the 400, I ran the prelims and the semis, holding just a little bit back. In the finals, I went all out but saved just a sliver, one of those incremental bits. Still, I won in 43.66, just a few tenths off the world record.

Now, 12 hours later, I was a 200-meter runner. The prelims and semis went the same way, bursting out in front and coasting in. Then the finals, legs pump-ing, back slightly arched, compact and low. I won in 19.83, and even though it was wind-aided, I'd shown that I could win both races in the same meet and still challenge the world records. I'd done something that had never been accomplished before, and the media took notice.

Next came the World Championships, in Göteborg, Sweden. This was an even bigger test. Besides the deeper competition, the World Championships con-tain four rounds in each race, unlike the U.S. Championships, which have only three. There was a slight gap between the end of the 400-meter races and the beginning of the 200. Coach Hart and I had figured that switching from one race to the other would be toughest physically, but we were surprised to find during the U.S. Championships that the real challenge was mental. Physically, it was challenging, but my times hadn't suffered at all. But I could see how switching back and forth might lead to mistakes. Now I'd have four heats in each race to think about and plan for, four chances for catastrophic failure.

I'd run well in Europe that season in both races, and in Göteborg I really wanted to show that I belonged in both races in Atlanta. I finessed my way through the first three rounds of the 400 and then tore out at 43.39 in the finals—still my fastest 400 meters ever. The 400 finals were at 7 P.M. and at 9 A.M. the next day was the preliminary round of the 200 meters. As I went over the technical checklist for the 200 in my mind, I could feel myself switching gears, and it was as if I were in a new meet altogether. Same strategy, same result. I ran my best time ever, 19.79—7 hundredths away from the world record.

I had done everything in my power. I'd shown that I could run and win both races with a few meters to spare. There was still no indication that the schedule makers would be swayed, but at least I'd made my case the only way I knew how: by winning.

Reporters are crazy about records, fascinated by what has never been done before. They hounded me with questions about the double, about whether I would attempt it in Atlanta. I have to think they posed a few to the IAAF as well. The double also seemed to interest the American public, which is usually notoriously uninterested in track and field.

Whatever the reason, the IAAF called the day after

the World Championships. It still wasn't promising anything, but it opened the door a crack, asking exactly what kind of schedule change I was requesting. Just a little time, I said. All I've ever needed is just the slightest bit of time.

1995 World Championships, Göteborg, Sweden.

TRAINING TIPS:
Perspective Leads
to Perseverance

1. STRIVE FOR BALANCE.

Don't let your goals smother your personal life, your relationships, or your health. Being successful without being well-rounded is a waste. Do something tangible: Add another hour of family time; go to the movies with your friends once a week.

2. REGAIN YOUR PERSPECTIVE.

This is one of those moments when you need to assess your journey so far. Give yourself time to think or to meditate or just to shut the machine off for a while.

3. LISTEN TO YOUR BODY.

It will tell you when you are going too fast or when you need something you're not getting. Burnout sets off alarms in your body as loud as those on a Mercedes in Los Angeles.

4. LOOK FOR NEW CHALLENGES.

Make sure they are the kind that keep you sharp, that exercise your mind and body and force you to continue using self-discipline, organization, and consistency. Those are transferable habits that need to be worked like muscles.

5. SIMPLIFY.

Trim the fat from your life and seek the motivation behind your chase, the 10-year-old's reasons you started on this journey in the first place.

Against 1992 Olympic Champion Michael Marsh (far left), at the 1996 Atlanta Grand Prix.

PRESSURE

GOLDEN SHOES

> Never excuse yourself to yourself.
>
> —Anonymous

It took me some time to

realize it, but I love pressure. If there is one thing that will really take you to another level of performance—to the plateau where your victories are measured in the blink of milli-seconds—it might be the ability to embrace pressure, to understand it, to draw it in, to make it your own and use it to your advantage.

I know that probably sounds nuts. We've been trained to think of pressure as the enemy, the unfair burden that holds us down. We see pressure as a compilation of the awful and the impossible, a sort of "greatest hits" of unreasonable expectations and complete bummers. Traffic is heavy, your boss expects a report you haven't finished yet, your girlfriend wants to talk about "the relationship," your rent is three months late, and your mechanic says you need a rebuild. Pressure. Think of all those people who fail because "the pressure got to them," or all those people who "buckled under the pressure," those who "can't take the pressure." We have constructed a flimsy city of clichés and excuses around that word, so it's no wonder people run away when "the pressure is on."

But to me, pressure is nothing more than the shadow of great opportunity. In that way, it is no more frightening than any shadow. Here's what I mean.

By the fall of 1995 I'd shown I could win both the 200 and the 400 in major Olympic-style events. Now I was just waiting to hear from the committee about the schedule. I began training harder than I ever had before. I'd learned quite a bit from my two attempts at running the double. I knew I needed to be stronger, so I increased my weight-room workouts and put another 10 pounds on my frame. I'd never weighed more than 175 pounds, but now I was 185 and I had successfully added strength and stamina without losing speed.

Now it was 1996 and the pressure was coming from everywhere.

There was the pressure of expectations from the media and the general public: Was he going to attempt the double? Was he going to fold the way he did in Barcelona? Would he fall on his face trying to do too much?

Financial pressure: Success meant higher fees for the professional meets. It meant a huge increase in my endorsements, as well as countless other opportunities. Failure meant I took a big cut in my meet fee, as I'd done after Barcelona. It wouldn't mean poverty, of course, but in the long run it could mean the loss of millions.

The pressure of my legacy: *No one* had ever done what I was attempting. Success meant that I became one of the most

Racing Darnell Hall (left), 1996 Indoor National Championships, Atlanta, Georgia.

celebrated track and field athletes of the 1990s. Failure meant that if I was remembered at all, it would be as someone who always choked in the big one.

Where did all of this pressure come from? The media? My family? Track fans? No. In the beginning it came from me. It came from the fact that I was attempting something great, something that *I* wanted. It came from me. There was great pressure because of the goals I had set. Why should I run from what I'd been chasing all these years? Since it was my goal, the thing I wanted, I couldn't hate pressure any more than I could hate my own goal, any more than I could hate myself. I can't deny the dragon I've been hunting all these years when I finally feel its breath.

That's what we forget sometimes, that we have set up our own challenges and the requisite pressure that goes with them. What do you want to do, pretend that your ambitions carry no consequences? Then why do it? Consequence and reward, like victory and loss, are tied too tightly together to pretend that you can have one without the other.

I said that pressure is just the shadow of great accomplishment and that's what I mean. Sometimes shadows are cast longer than the thing itself, and pressure can seem like that, more weighty than the accomplishment it's reflecting. But like a shadow, there is really no substance there. Move into the light and shadows fade. Move into a shadow's way and you can block it with your own.

I know, this is all very ethereal. That's why there are concrete things you can do with the pressure that accumulates for you. But first you have to work at abandoning the mind games that we all play, the little tricks we spring on ourselves to try to ward off pressure, a long list of silly superstitions that are no more useful than wearing garlic to scare off vampires.

For instance, there's the I'm-the-underdog game. I've seen this from many track and field athletes, most recently from Frank Fredericks of Namibia, one of the top sprinters and nicest guys in the world. When Frank beat me once a few weeks before the Olympics, he was suddenly cast in the role of favorite in the 200 meters by reporters looking to build suspense. He reacted in a way that shocked me. To get the pressure off himself, he said I should be the favorite, that he had almost no chance of beating me.

Even if I believed that going into a race, I would never say it. As soon as you squirm out from under the expectations of winning, it's nearly impossible to win. If you expect to finish second, that's where you will finish. If you tell your friends they are smarter than you are, they *will get* better grades. It doesn't take much for us to believe our own words.

Then there's the this-isn't-important game. I've also heard this from track and field athletes, who insist that running is second to their singing career or their many business investments. "It doesn't matter if I lose, I've got all these other things going." Or they might say that track is just a business and as long as they're making money, winning isn't important.

If that were true, they would be on Wall Street working as stockbrokers, or they would devote their lives to singing. Instead, it's just one of those tricks to excuse losing before you

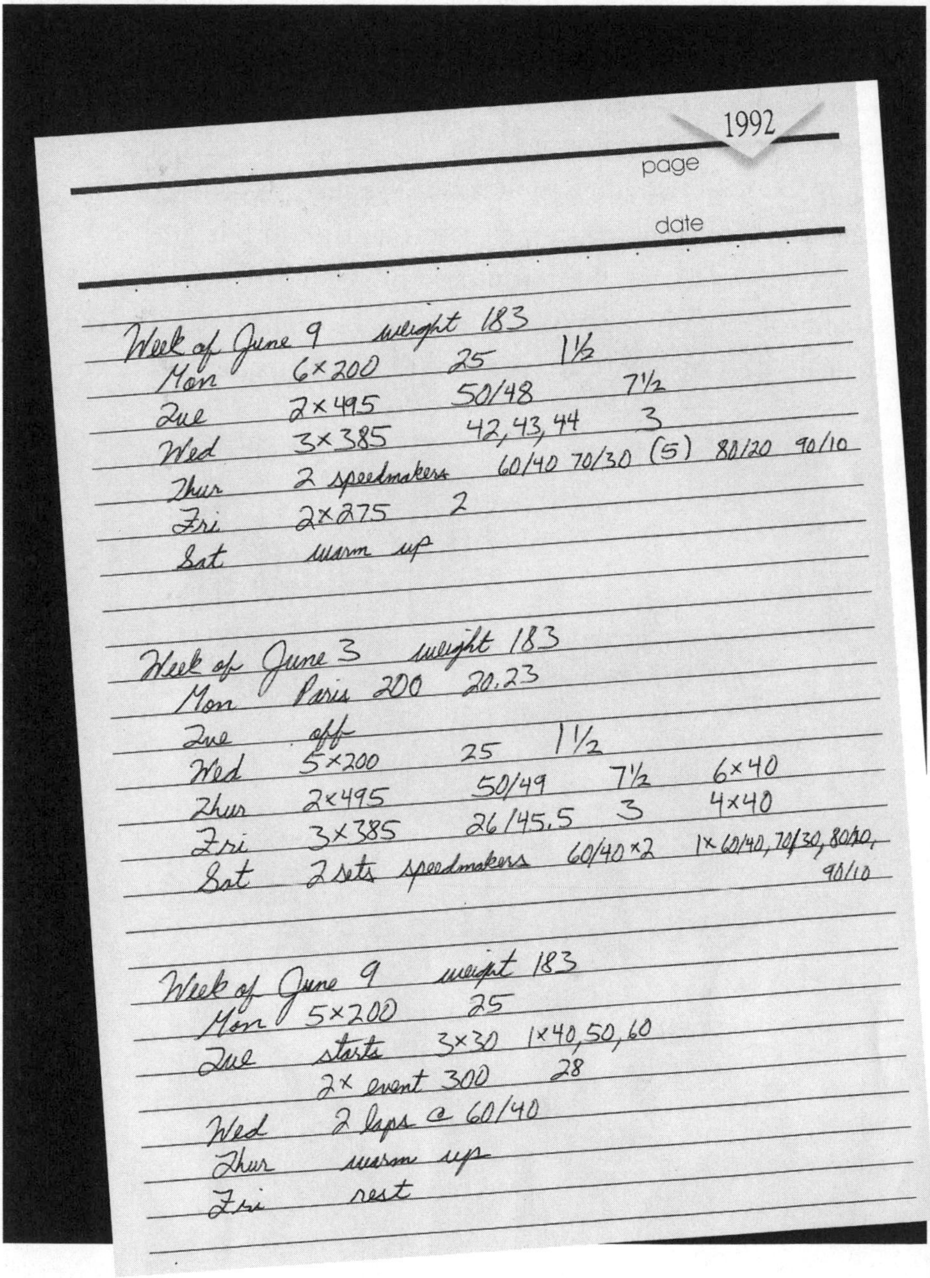

Week of June 9   weight 183
Mon   6×200   25   1½
Tue   2×495   50/48   7½
Wed   3×385   42,43,44   3
Thur   2 speedmakers   60/40 70/30 (5) 80/20 90/10
Fri   2×275   2
Sat   warm up

Week of June 3   weight 183
Mon   Paris 200   20.23
Tue   off
Wed   5×200   25   1½
Thur   2×495   50/49   7½   6×40
Fri   3×385   26/45.5   3   4×40
Sat   2 sets speedmakers 60/40×2   1× 60/40, 70/30, 80/20,
                                              90/10

Week of June 9   weight 183
Mon   5×200   25
Tue   starts   3×30   1×40,50,60
        2× event 300   28
Wed   2 laps @ 60/40
Thur   warm up
Fri   rest

Another page from my training journal.

ever lose. "Oh, it's OK. I didn't need to win anyway." We all need to win, and if you can't admit that something like the Olympics is important—if you can't admit that your senior prom is important, or that your first job interview is important—then you're just kidding yourself. Minimizing the risks does nothing but minimize you and the things you can accomplish.

Finally, there's the this-is-like-any-other-race game. You can substitute your own word at the end (this-is-like-any-other-date or project or test). What it means is that you're trying to deny the pressure, to ignore it and hope it goes away by pretending that this date or project or test or race isn't as big as it is.

What a monumental waste! If this race is no bigger than any other, then why do it? Why train as hard as you have? Why work so late at the office if this account is no different from any other?

In all these instances, what you should be doing is embracing the pressure. Will your wedding day be one of the biggest days of your life? You bet it will be! You should have great expectations for it, prepare well for it, and plan to do everything you can to make those dreams true. And if something goes wrong anyway? Pretending it's not important isn't going to lessen the sting when the minister passes out and knocks over two bridesmaids.

All those mind games will do is give you a ready-made excuse before you ever get started. They will allow you to slack off in your studying ("School isn't really my priority anyway"), abandon your discipline ("It doesn't matter if I do 20 more sit-ups"), and not ask the girl you love to the prom ("Aw, it's just another dance").

It's quite simple really. It's about never fooling yourself, about not wasting time and energy on self-deception. If you are

operating at as high a level as you'd like, if you have adopted a sprinter's training and your goals are now just split-seconds away, then you are too efficient to play such games with yourself.

For instance, before important meets like the Olympics, I have a meeting with my coach, Clyde Hart, and we go over the things I have to do that day. Coach is a lot like me in that he doesn't believe in playing games. He doesn't give me pep talks or tell lame jokes to try easing the pressure on me. We talk business—the specific things I have to remember for this particular race. He knows that—like him—I thrive on the pressure and it would be silly to try to relieve it. I like to know that I am on a course toward something worthwhile. The higher the expectations, the higher I usually perform. I'm someone who likes to see the long shadow of the thing I'm about to attempt.

So, first you recognize the pressure for what it is: a reflection of your own ambition. Then you draw the pressure in, acknowledge that you'd like to sell the most carpet in September, that you'd like to win the trip to Germany. And then, most important, you claim the pressure for yourself, internalize it, and make it yours.

You do that by taking outside pressure and forcing it inside, taking the expectations of others and replacing them with your own expectations. You have probably realized by now that I'm someone who likes to have control of the things around me. Pressure is a tough thing to control, and the only way I know to control pressure is to make it your own.

"Yes, I expect to win." "I'd like to get an A on that test." "I really need to get that job." "I put a lot of work into this. If I lose, the world won't end, but you bet I'll be disappointed." Announcing your intentions and the stakes is the best way to reclaim the pressure. You don't always need to announce it to anyone but yourself, but you need to be honest about it, to admit the things that are at stake. Pretending they're not at stake doesn't make them any less important or make their loss any less raw, it only makes you less sharp, less focused, more willing to give up before you ever start.

I guess that's the bottom line for a lot of this stuff, for me and for other successful people I know: honesty. You need to be completely honest with yourself, to be aware of what you can do, why you succeed and why you fail. You need to honestly assess your work habits, your weaknesses, and the pressures aligning with you.

And sometimes, the only way to reclaim the outside pressure is to top it, to do something so audacious that the pressure to succeed falls squarely back onto your shoulders. Something symbolic and confident. Something like running in the Olympics in gold shoes. All the pressure that was beginning to build for me as the 1996 Olympics approached still fit easily into those shiny 2-ounce specially made Nikes. After all, what failure could be worse after Barcelona than losing in such bold footwear? How could you look more stupid than to be the guy accepting a bronze medal in gold shoes?

OUT OF THE BLOCKS

List the pressures.

Get out that pen again. Pressure is just another factor that we can control. But first you have to figure out what the specific pressures are and where they are coming from. Separate the pressures that you need from the ones that result from miscommunication or unrealistic expectations. Does your boss expect a report before you can realistically finish it? Talk to him. Does your boss expect the report in such a short amount of time that you will barely be able to make it? Get it done. Figure it out. Does your family expect more than you can give? Or do they expect what you yourself would consider your best?

OTHER VOICES

At the end of every hard day, people find some reason
to believe.
—*Bruce Springsteen, twentieth-century American singer*

Starting from zero, got nothing to losc.
—*Tracy Chapman, twentieth-century American singer*

To win without risk is to triumph without glory.
—*Pierre Corneille, nineteenth-century French playwright*

The sigh he makes is deep, a hungry air-take for the
strength and perseverance all life . . . takes.
—*Toni Morrison, twentieth-century American novelist*

In anything at all, perfection is finally attained not
when there is no longer anything to add, but when
there is no longer anything to take away.
—*Antoine de Saint-Exupéry, twentieth-century French novelist*

BUILDING PRESSURE

GOLDEN SHOES

I got word in December of 1995 that they were going to try changing the schedule of the Atlanta games for me. In March of 1996 they made the announcement: they were changing because of the overwhelming interest in whether or not I could accomplish the double. It hung over the first part of the season like a brewing storm.

Then came the Olympic trials in Atlanta, a month before the games. In the 400-meter, I shot out from lane 5 in the middle of a thick pack. By the midpoint of the race I was in second place; 100 meters later I had a half-second lead on my nearest rival. I finished in 43.44, a half-second better than Butch Reynolds. I was halfway to qualifying for the double.

In the 200 meter, Carl Lewis was out of the blocks first. I was out in 18 hundredths of a second, fifth fastest in my heat. Again from lane 5 I cranked around the curve and when I emerged from it I was alone. I crossed the finish line, looked over my shoulder and, prefiguring what would happen in the Olympics, saw a new world record on the big digital clock. It read 19.66.

The oldest world record in track and field—dating back to 1979—had fallen by 6 hundredths of a second. I celebrated, posed for pictures next to the clock, and ran my victory lap. Everything was going according to plan. And there is nothing I like better than that.

With the end of the trials, the attention and pressure were incredible. The companies that I already

Swatch Scan'o'Vision of the 200-meter final, 1996 Olympic Trials, Atlanta, Georgia.

ch□ swatch□ swatch□ swatch□ swc
NG TIMING TIMING TIMING TIM

sults:						Windspeed: + 1.7 m/s	
ik	Lane	Bib				Finish time	Start
	Number	Number					Reaction
1.	5	379	Michael JOHNSON		NIK	19.658	0.183
2.	6	830	Jeff WILLIAMS		UNA	20.024	0.205
3.	4	555	Michael MARSH		SMT	20.034	0.201
4.	3	350	Ramon CLAY		NFS	20.080	0.166
5.	1	553	Carl LEWIS		SMT	20.194	0.140
6.	2	340	Alvis WHITTED		NCS	20.304	0.185
7.	8	550	Floyd HEARD		SMT	20.340	0.163
8.	7	842	Kevin LITTLE		USW	20.384	0.174

endorsed were making plans and taking up even more of my time; media requests came six, seven a day; the networks and news magazines prepared profiles of me.

How would I handle all that media pressure? Embrace it. Add to it. Ask Nike for several pairs of gold shoes. Launch an Internet Web site. Agree to write an Olympic column for *USA Today*. And tell *Sports Illustrated*, "What this means is history. There are two household names in the history of track and field—Jesse Owens and Carl Lewis. I'm in position to be the third."

There. Now THAT'S pressure.

Soon after, I received a letter from Jesse Owens's widow. She wished me luck and wrote that I reminded her of her late husband in the way I ran and the way I carried myself off the track. The letter meant so much to me. I carried it with me to Atlanta.

A few last tune-ups: I ran three European races before the Olympics. The first was a 400-meter race in Lausanne, Switzerland. I won easily. Next came a 200-meter race in Oslo, Norway. Frank Fredericks was running extremely well when we met on the track in Oslo. I had just run that 400 in Lausanne, and I was smack in the middle of switching from the 400-meter Michael to the 200-meter Michael. I knew that to beat Frank I'd need to run a great curve, so as we wedged into the blocks, I concentrated on the curve, on the technical things I needed to do to get up and around the curve, to fling myself out into the lead.

But with the start, I made a tiny mistake, one of

those sprinter's fractions. I was thinking so much about the curve—the second zone of the race—that I didn't think about the first. Instead of reacting to the gun, I waited and got left in the blocks. The other guys were still churning, and I started the race in a hole that I couldn't quite crawl out of. Frank edged me at the finish line: 19.85 to 19.83.

Another helping of pressure, anyone?

Now, two weeks before the Olympics, I had lost a race. It was a tough time for me because I hate to lose. My mistake had been completely avoidable. Now, all of a sudden, the media had a new story: Michael Johnson is vulnerable! He's human!

I could have told them that. Any runner can lose any race any time. That is the other edge of my great confidence, the knowledge (which I've learned firsthand) that anything can go wrong at any time. Still, I was surprised when some writers began to say that Frank Fredericks might be the favorite to win the 200 in Atlanta. So, two days later, I ran the 200 again, in Stockholm against Ato Bolden of Trinidad and Tobago, who was the other person I knew I had to beat in Atlanta and the eventual Olymic bronze medalist. I won that race in 19.77 on a very tough track.

Now, for me, the issue was over. I wouldn't make that mistake in Atlanta. I wouldn't make that mistake ever again. For me, the proof was in the statistics. I was running 19.6s and 19.7s, and even when Frank beat me, it was in 19.8. If he'd beaten me with a 19.6, I'd have been worried, but now I fully expected to win.

It is what my training and performance have been about over the last ten years. I have arrived at a place where, if I'm capable of doing something, I fully expect to do it. That is the pinnacle of a sprinter's training: to be so consistent and refined in your performance that you always expect to do your best. To know your body so well that you can guess, within hundredths of a second, the time you will run.

For any of us, the pressure builds and builds until the defining moment, and that is the time I crave. When I slide into the blocks, I don't care if the whole world expects me to win. I hope they do. Because I expect to win.

TRAINING TIPS:
Pressure

1. DON'T PRETEND THERE IS NO PRESSURE.

That's what people often try to do, but it doesn't work. You don't want to play mind games with yourself. Honesty is the only way.

2. DON'T USE IT AS AN EXCUSE.

The pressure you blame today for a failure will show up again tomorrow. Find the technical reasons for your missed free-throws, the grammatical errors in your essay test. Those are the real problems.

3. TRACE PRESSURE TO ITS ROOT.

Outside pressures almost always come about because you've put yourself in a position to do something memorable. Pressure springs from you. It is impressive, a reflection of your own ambition.

4. MAKE IT YOURS.

Pressure is like anything else. If you control it, you can make it work for you instead of against you. Realize that the pressure to succeed comes from within and then apply it yourself.

5. USE IT AS MOTIVATION.

If it comes from within, then pressure can be a tremendous motivator. If you can work under pressure, then the more that is at stake, the better you will perform. That's all you can ask of yourself.

1996 Olympic Trials, Atlanta, Georgia.

PERFORMANCE

THE DANGER ZONE

9

> Time is not the click of the
> clock. It is the everlasting now.
> —ANONYMOUS

I arrived in Atlanta, Georgia,

on July 18, 1996, the night before the opening ceremonies of
the Centennial Olympic Games. I had almost a week before my
first race, so I didn't bring any running shoes, no uniforms,
nothing to work out in. For a couple of days, I would be like
most of the other people in Atlanta, just a fan. All around me
the city swelled and buzzed, streets bursting with impatient
traffic, hotel lobbies filled with expectant fans and intense athletes, all with that general restless thrill of the Olympics.

I'd already been through the opening ceremonies in
Barcelona and had felt the pride stir in my chest as we paraded
into the stadium beneath the American flag. Now I was older
and more mature, completely focused on the races I would
run. But I was profoundly moved to be competing for America

in front of American fans; to march alongside the athletes I'd trained with and competed against; to watch the great boxing champion Muhammad Ali shudder as he held the torch to light the Olympic flame.

After the opening ceremonies, I returned to Dallas to train for a few more days and watched the first days of Olympic competition on television.

And then I came back to Atlanta, this time with my gold shoes, my workout clothes, my uniforms, and the steely-eyed look I wear to meets. This time I came to take care of business, to do the thing I'd set as a goal, the thing I'd promised myself. This time, everything was in place and I came simply to perform.

Performance may not be a word you associate with the things you are trying to achieve. It may be hard to think of a job at the accounting firm as "performing," but I think that is where our success lies—in performances; in short, infrequent bursts of opportunity where we are essentially out there alone, on a stage or a track or in a meeting or a classroom. In other words, your everyday work at the accounting firm might not be described as performing, but more like working out, rehearsing, training. But when you are given the responsibility of handling the firm's biggest client at tax time, what else is that but a chance to perform in front of others, a quick opportunity to display your natural ability, your hard work, and your ability to improvise, to think on your feet. What is a final exam but a 400-meter race—an instant test of your ability and preparation.

That is the magic of a sprinter's training—perfect preparation for those short, wildly important, do-or-die bursts.

They start, as everything in athletics does, with the mind.

That might surprise people, coming from an athlete. There is a misconception that all athletes are naturally physical and

1996 Olympic Trials, Atlanta, Georgia.

distrust anything that doesn't come from sheer muscle memory. The great Yankee catcher Yogi Berra summed up that kind of thinking: "How can you think and hit at the same time?" There is the perception that sports are best left to those who don't think too much, that the mind only gets in the way of truly great athletes.

Of course that's not true at all. Sure, you can accomplish a lot with nothing but physical gifts and intuitive reflex. But the mind is the only place that can comprehend the truly great, and it's the best weapon any of us has when it comes time to perform.

It's the day of the bar exam. It's your wedding day, your high school reunion, your once-a-year job evaluation. Everything you need to perform—*to do exactly what you are capable of doing*—is in your mind: concentration and planning.

They are like supports holding each other up. One, concentration, is the complete and intense focus on your goal—the Danger Zone, as I like to think of it. The other is the on-board computer checklist, running through the technical aspects of whatever you are about to do, the steps you're going to take when the test begins. All you can ask of your body is to perform as well as it ever has during your training; all you can ask of your mind is the same.

I don't believe in that sports cliché—giving 110 percent. It's foolish to hope constantly for better performances than we are capable of producing, for the ability to surprise ourselves in big situations.

I believe that on our best day, we are capable of doing only what we are capable of doing, and that's what we should be shooting for. Most days, far from reaching 110 percent, most of us struggle to hit 50 percent. Be honest with yourself. How much drive and creativity have you been putting into your job? Imagine every day at the office using 80 or 90 percent of your natural ability, 80 or 90 percent of your self-discipline, 80 or 90 percent of your determination. You would clean up!

I want you to work the way I have, to arrive at a place where you are running your own particular races at 95, 96, 97 percent efficiency. And every once in a while, as with me in Atlanta, you might come within a whisper of the very limits of your ability, within sight of perfection.

Here is what my mind is doing in the minutes before a race. First: concentration. I have learned to cut out all the unnecessary thoughts—the circular fears and hesitations that get in the way. I don't pace around the blocks imagining what might happen if I lose. I don't try to psyche myself up. If I didn't want to win this race, I wouldn't be out there, so there is no need to give myself any more motivation, to psyche myself. I don't visualize the race or daydream about winning. I simply concentrate. I concentrate on the tangible—on the track, on the race, on the blocks, on the things I have to do.

And I use concentration to access the plan I've set up. I've heard people say that I look possessed in the blocks before a race, my eyebrows cut into sharp V's, my mouth drawn tight, and my eyes clear, focused on some point far off, unblinking.

I must be thinking about destruction, some people think, about killing my opponents.

1996 Olympic Trials, Atlanta, Georgia.

| | | | 43.4 | 43.5 | 43.6 | 44.3 | 44.4 | 44.5 | 44.6 | 44.7 | 44.8 | 44.9 | 4 |

Results:

Rank	Lane Number	Bib Number			Finish time	Start Reacti
1.	4	2370	Michael JOHNSON	USA	43.484	0.254
2.	3	1469	Roger BLACK	GBR	44.401	0.205
3.	2	2300	Davis KAMOGA	UGA	44.521	0.264
4.	1	2357	Alvin HARRISON	USA	44.620	0.237
5.	8	1512	Iwan THOMAS	GBR	44.691	0.365
6.	5	1745	Roxbert MARTIN	JAM	44.822	0.283
7.	6	1737	Davian CLARKE	JAM	44.983	0.348

Mentally, I enter what I call the danger zone, a place inside of myself with an incredible pool of focus, where I become acutely aware of my opponents and the fact that they are trying to keep me from winning. But I think of my opponents only for a moment. Most of the time, when I am glowering and my eyes are challenging the world, I am simply planning, going over some technical checklist: "React, don't wait for the gun. Stay low. Get up around the corner." I imagine myself becoming leaner and more efficient. For that one moment, I am a machine, perfectly designed and programmed for the task ahead of me. Hard, cold steel.

Swatch Scan '0' Vision of 1996 Olympic 400-meter final, Atlanta, Georgia

Last-minute planning for a performance is really just an extension of the planning that begins when you set your first goal. All along, you should have been aware of each step. You've listed each technique and tip that you need to get from goal A to goal B. You've broken each of those plans into smaller plans and written those down as well. You've drawn the perfect map for where you are going. Now you just have to follow it. Your performance plan is like that, a series of reminders and tips, a checklist for your on-board computer on the day of the race or the test or the class reunion.

Finally, the gun will go off. Or you'll sit down with your two No. 2 pencils and begin taking the SATs. Or you'll show up at your high school reunion wearing a dress that didn't fit two weeks earlier.

Finally, the fun will begin. The machine will be gone, and the training and planning and work will support the human being. When I am running, the checklist still scrolls through my mind and the concentration remains intact, but deep inside I'm a 10-year old again. It's just a foot race, after all. Planning and concentration are the keys that free you to have fun and to perform at your highest level, with the best results. Planning and concentration strip away everything on the fringes, and all that's left is the joy that you get from your job or your family or your hobby.

In Atlanta, the early rounds of the 400 meters went as well as I had planned: short bursts and then cruising into the finish, saving just enough for the next race. I became more confident with each stride, each glance back at my opponents and at the clock.

After the 400 quarterfinal, I went to bed early to be ready for my next race. About 3 A.M. on July 27, I got a telephone call from my brother. Had I heard the bomb? It had gone off in the park right across from my hotel, during a rock concert. No, I said, I hadn't heard anything.

Like the rest of America, I sat up that night watching the aftermath on television. A woman, a mother, was killed by the blast, and a man suffered a fatal heart attack. I called a few people to make sure they were OK and to tell them I was OK. But mostly I just watched in disbelief and sorrow.

The next morning, everyone was still in a daze. Should we continue competing in the face of this? I talked earlier about perspective, and to imagine a young girl without her mother put everything in a new perspective. The results of races and gymnastics routines seemed far less important than human life.

In the end, we decided—all of Atlanta decided—that the best thing was to compete. In 1972, the Munich Olympics had been hijacked by terrorism, and the images we have from those games are not of competition but of the horrible struggle and deaths of so many Israeli athletes at the hands of terrorists.

No one wanted that to be the legacy of Atlanta. No one wanted the terror to have the last word. With the deepest respect for the victims, I think everyone wanted to push on, to sear a different set of images on these Olympic games. In the shadow of terror and death, I am not brash enough to think that a foot race is the most important thing in the world. But I would be lying if I didn't admit that it was the thing I had come for. It was the culmination of ten years devoted to incremental progress, ten years of trying to slay a dragon that moved ahead of me in milliseconds, ten years of training and focus that had gained me all of a second-and-a-half in real time. It was time. And now, more than ever before, I was ready.

OUT OF THE BLOCKS

Plan to perform.

You've set intricate goals, drawn efficient plans, and now, with everything on the line, you can't expect to rely just on instinct. Performance time is when you need your planning skills the most. First, they give you something to focus on, tangible steps to take to get to your goal. They give you a vehicle for your concentration and the incredible mental power you can put into any task. This is the wrong time to leave things to chance.

A willing mind makes a light foot.
—*Thomas Fuller,* seventeeth-century English clergyman

A conqueror is like a cannonball. He cannot stop on his own accord. He must go on until he runs down or hits something.
—*Leonard Cooper,* twentieth-century American historian

There is no pain in the wound received in the moment of victory.
—*Publilius Syrus,* first-century B.C. Roman writer

Life only demands from you the strength you possess. Only one feat is possible: not to have run away.
—*Dag Hammarskjöld,* twentieth-century Swedish diplomat

PERFORMING

THE DANGER ZONE

At first I don't visualize anything. I leave the hotel and go out to the track to warm up an hour before I am to run. Headphones slide over my ears—the familiar rhythm and raw power of rap music. My eyes close. I am calm and yet I am at the edge of something, the adrenaline beginning to well up already.

Earlier on the day of competition, I have met with my coach, Clyde Hart, and we've gone over every outstanding detail. Where will I go between races? Will I stay in the stadium or return to the warm-up track? When will I begin my final warm-up? I want every detail considered and planned. When I'm in the zone, I don't want to come out to figure out how I'm going to get to the stadium or where I should stand.

I am deep inside. There is no fear in here. No second-guessing. None of the games that we play with ourselves. My self-discipline has cut most of that fat away and whatever is left is no match for my confidence. I am in the best shape here. I am the best performer here. I am in control of what happens.

I stretch, run a few starts at the warm-up track. I run with my mind completely focused on the technique, the hundreds of muscles that will join to create each stride. High legs, quick strides, arms pumping. Nothing has been left to chance in my training. Now I am as confident in my preparation as I am in my ability. Now, for me, they are one and the same.

The crowds in Atlanta are amazing. A full stadium, 80,000 people, for preliminary races! And now, in the finals of the 400 meters, the stadium is again full, cameras flashing, people screaming. They are so much a part of what I want to do, so vital to the performance, but I won't interact with them until after the race, during my victory lap.

The headphones come off. The warm-ups come off.

There are Roger Black of Great Britain and Calvin Harrison of the United States, nice men and great athletes. But today, they and five other men want something that is mine, and I will not let them have it.

Focus on the track. It is one lane wrapping once around the inside of this stadium. The track. The crowd fades away and the other athletes disappear and now it's just me and this one lane. I have done this so many times in my life. I have run this race so many times that now I focus on its familiar rhythms. There are four zones. The start, steadier and less manic than in the 200. It's possible to have a slow 400 start and still win. That doesn't happen in the 200. The second zone, finding a comfortable, fast stride to get you through the first curve and the middle portion of the race. In the third zone, building into your kick, coming around that last curve. And the last zone, where you just hold on and scramble to the finish.

I go through each of the zones and the things I want to do, the places I want to be. I back into the blocks like a rocket eased onto a launch pad. It's the

USA

Rec. MICHAEL JOHNSON
LANE 4
12701

Panasonic

The 1996 Olympic Stadium, with
the big-screen television.

most uncomfortable position in the world—tensed, poised, bent over a two-point stance. My eyes focus on the track beneath me, and then, slowly, they rise until I'm focused on some point down there, exactly 400 meters away.

The checklists are still running, and once more—in a flash—I go over the things I want to do . . . the things I expect to do. Now the voice fades and I'm ready, channeling everything into pure movement and flow . . .

Bang!

What does it feel like, to move this fast? That's the question I hear after all the polite ones have been asked. Yeah, but what does it feel like?

It feels great.

Some people might say there is nothing sexy about planning, nothing terribly exciting about setting goals, working toward them, and arriving.

But in truth it's the best feeling in the world. It's the buzz of human accomplishment and the only way any of us can touch greatness. I am propelled down that track, pushed by ten years of desire, hard work, and commitment, pushed a little faster by the screams and the flashes and the spectacle, pushed even faster by the finely tuned athletes on all sides of me who are chasing the same thing. The air explodes with each step, and the finish line is in front of me and my arms fly out, a smile comes, and then I notice the crowd, my parents, and people who have never met me and yet are screaming themselves hoarse to cheer me on. I run a victory lap; give both of my golden shoes to my parents. I did it.

They place a gold medal over my shoulders and play the American national anthem. Of course, there were no guarantees that I would ever get here. I set out on this journey knowing that. And now I let everything wash over me. Tears spill out of my eyes but I don't blink them away. The 10-year-old wants to enjoy every moment of this, to revel in the beauty of something dreamed, something planned, something accomplished. There is magic in that after all.

TRAINING TIPS:
Performance

1. DON'T BE AFRAID TO PERFORM.
You have worked harder than anyone. You have committed yourself to this goal. Now don't back away from the pressure and the people watching.

2. USE YOUR SECRET WEAPON: YOUR MIND.
Your power to concentrate and follow a plan is incredible and, unfortunately, too often untapped. As strong as my legs are, it is my mind that has made me a champion.

3. BE CALM AND EFFICIENT.
Don't try to psyche yourself up. You'll only succeed in psyching yourself out. You have worked to be unflappable and not waste a single movement or thought. That is how you will succeed, not by beating your head against a wall and primal screaming.

4. GO.
Whatever your goal, there is a release point where you simply do it. There comes a time when you have to jump off the diving board. Practice quick release and instant action. This is no time to debate yourself.

5. ENJOY.

This is what your journey has been about. Relax and remember what it is you love about this.

EPILOGUE

A day and a half after win-

ning the 400, I lined up for my first two rounds of the 200 meters. I ran well and was able to cruise to the win in both, but the strain on me physically was beginning to show. My left Achilles tendon was sore, the tendon behind my left knee was weakening, and my sacroiliac joint needed constant adjustment. I ached in the morning after those first two rounds, but I still felt confident. Two more races to go. I was relieved and free of the burdens of Barcelona after the 400 victory, but if anything the pressure had increased. Olympic officials had changed the schedule just for me, just so I could accomplish this thing, and now the biggest race of my life was still ahead. Even with the aches and pains, I felt alive, ready to attack the 200.

I had won the 400 meters going away, in 43.49 seconds, two-tenths of a second from the world record. Immediately afterward, reporters asked if I was disappointed that I hadn't broken the record or if I had held back to conserve energy for the

200. I explained that I run as fast as I can and that the gold medal was more important than any records. There is so much focus on world records that, as an athlete, it can become disheartening. You win a gold medal, beat the best in the world, and the first thing they ask you is why you didn't break the world record.

People have no idea how much it takes to get this far, the tiny incremental steps you have to take, the microimprovements and huge sacrifices. I first came within sight of the 200-meter record in 1990. From that time on, in the back of my mind, I always wanted to run faster in the 200 than anyone ever had. I was always mentioned as someone who could break the 200-meter record. But it took me seven years of complete and total devotion to this sport, seven years of victory, loss, and more victory, before I finally broke the record during the Olympic trials. That record had stood since 1979—seventeen years, longer than any record in track and field. An entire generation of athletes—almost two—had come and gone in the time it took someone to break that record.

We are spoiled. World records are so incredibly rare, so difficult to achieve, that our expectations of them are somewhat unreal. To set a world record, everything has to be perfect. The surface of the track, the weather, the crowd, and especially the competition have to be near-perfect. If it were that easy to break world records, it wouldn't take seventeen years to do it.

Still, when I look toward the next four years, toward the end of my competitive running career, the world record in the 400 looms large ahead of me. I know that one day—perhaps soon—the track will be right, the crowd will be excited, the

THE PACE OF PROGRESS: THE WORLD RECORD IN THE 200 METERS

Three times in this century a runner has significantly lowered the world record in the 200 meters by a third of a second or more (names in **boldface**). In seventy years, only nine men have broken the official world record.

21.0 Helmet Kornig, Germany, 1928
      (Two others later tied)
20.7 **Jesse Owens***, USA, 1936
      (Two others later tied)
20.6 Andrew Stanfield, USA, 1952
      (Four others later tied)
20.5 Stonewall Johnson, USA, 1960
      (20.75 electronic; Three others later tied)
20.36 Henry Carr, USA, 1964
      (Electronically timed)
20.14 Tommie Smith, USA, 1967
      (20.26 in a 220-yard race)
19.83 **Tommie Smith***, USA, 1968
      (Earlier times of 20.0 and 19.9 ruled unofficial)
19.8 Donald Quarrie, Jamaica, 1975
      (Handtimed)
19.72 Pietro Mennes, Italy, 1979
      (Held record 17 years, the longest held record ever)
19.66 Michael Johnson, USA, 1996
      (U.S. Olympic Trials)
19.32 **Michael Johnson***, USA, 1996

* Record broken during the Olympics

competition will be strong, and I will make a run at 43.29. It is one of the dragons I have left to slay, and I know one day we will meet. I'll be ready.

But even if I don't come out on top that time, there are other goals, other dragons, that don't exist on the track. I hope to become more involved in the marketing, business, and player decisions with the NBA's Dallas Mavericks, of which I'm a minority owner. I've also been blessed with other business and marketing opportunities since the Olympics. Chances are that

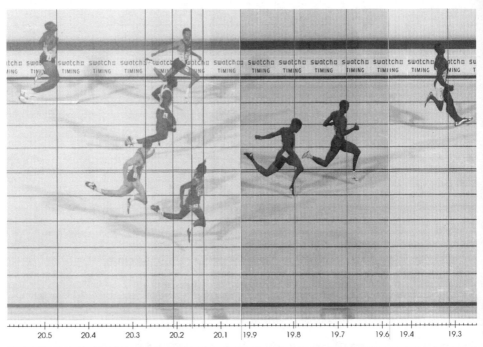

| 20.5 | 20.4 | 20.3 | 20.2 | 20.1 | 19.9 | 19.8 | 19.7 | 19.6 | 19.4 | 19.3 |

Results:							Windspeed: + 0.4 m/s	
Rank	Lane Number	Bib Number					Finish time	Start Reaction
1.	3	2370	Michael JOHNSON			USA	19.313	0.161
2.	5	1962	Frank FREDERICKS			NAM	19.679	0.200
3.	6	2288	Ato BOLDON			TRI	19.796	0.208
4.	8	1098	Obadele THOMPSON			BAR	20.138	0.202
5.	2	2405	Jeff WILLIAMS			USA	20.165	0.182
6.	4	1272	Ivan GARCIA			CUB	20.208	0.229
7.	7	1113	Patrick STEVENS			BEL	20.270	0.151
8.	1	2375	Michael MARSH			USA	20.471	0.167

Swatch Scan'O' Vision, 200-meter final, 1996 Olympic Games, Atlanta, Georgia.

I won't be the best businessman in the world (usually the most we can expect is far less than that), but I will approach the business world the way I run, with the same order and passion. I will set goals and make plans, work with discipline, and embrace pressure. I also think I'll probably be successful.

I hope to get married and start a family, although those kind of goals need a different kind of planning. There are limits even to the things that confidence and self-discipline can accomplish. For instance, this is not a goal that will work: "Memo to self: Fall in love, April 1998." Some things in our lives are more like fishing: you wait patiently and you know what to do when the time comes for action. I'm really looking forward to my own family, and I hope I can be as good a parent as mine were. I won't push my children into athletics. They will, however, learn the value of the things I have learned to value: self-reliance, planning, consistency, and an overriding passion for whatever it is that you do.

And what about my running career? When it's over, I will miss the joy of competing, but I don't think I will miss my running career. In many ways, it's like any job—a long succession of repeated tasks and hard work, an obstacle course of ambition, greed, and politics. But that's just the career part. The running has been wonderful, and I will undoubtedly miss the feeling of flying down that track, the days when I was the fastest man in the world.

I plan to run in the 2000 Olympics in Sydney, Australia. Will I defend my double there? I don't know. It's too early to say. Will I try to break the 400-meter record there? Again, it's too early to set those kinds of goals.Perhaps the 2000 Olympics will most likely be my last track meet. I will be 32 and, I hope, still at my competitive best. That's how I want to go out, with the dangerous look and the gold shoes still striking fear in hearts of athletes who run against me.

There's a chance I might never accomplish anything as incredible as my double in Atlanta, especially my record-setting 200 meters. But I'm not disappointed by that. I'm emboldened.

My other goals will probably be more humble than the ones I was able to set as a runner. Sometimes they will be more like the goal I set for my finite math class in college: just survive.

But I will forever carry the feeling of victory, and it will serve me in whatever I do. I have seen what is possible and what can happen with the joining of spirit and body. I have seen with amazing clarity the capability of one man performing with focus, efficiency, and fury, with the confidence of someone who has worked as hard as he possibly can. I have looked the dragon square in his eyes and I have laid him out flat.

1996 Olympic Games, Atlanta, Georgia

1996 Olympic Games, Atlanta, Georgia.

THE DRAGON

Block out the pain.

The morning of the 200 final, I know that a few minor aches and twinges are as much a waste of my energy as second-guessing. I only have time now for those things that will help me.

I won my semifinal in 20.27; Frankie Fredericks won his in 19.98. Frankie also finished second in the 100 meters to Donovan Bailey, who set a new world record. Clearly he is running at his peak, as I am. I'm wary of him, but I'm also glad that we're coming together at our best because I know what it's going to take to beat him and I know that I will have to run as fast as I ever have.

In the blocks, I lean forward on the thumb and forefinger of each hand. Let the others fight off the pressure here. I welcome it like my best friend, and its huge questions only reinforce my will: Is this the race of your life? It is. Do you have a lot to lose? Everything. Do you have to win? Yes.

But those thoughts are merely flashes, and the ones that interest me are technical. A computer-assisted, graphically enhanced model of how to run 200 meters plays in my brain, and I go over each step, from gun to gold. I'm ready. It's right there in front of me and I have stared long enough into its eyes. For ten years I have stared at this beast and I have hunted it without knowing if I would ever get close enough.

1996 Olympic Games, Atlanta, Georgia.

Focused, tense, I wait in the blocks. Flinch slightly, involuntarily. My entire being is waiting for that bang, and when it comes I move with it, out of the blocks in 16 hundredths, and even with the stumble on the third step I'm flying. I catch Frankie at 80 meters and there's no one else to chase from that point on. Only my goals, my core, the dragon I've come to slay.

At the end, my hamstring screaming almost as loud as the crowd, I'm chasing only the chase itself. Cross the finish line. Turn. Yellow bulbs arranged in a pattern of numbers on the red stadium clock: 200 m . . . 19.32.

Sports Illustrated would report later that experts and statisticians had predicted such times in the 200 meters . . . in the year 2020! I have skipped ahead twenty-five years, skipped the 19.5s and the 19.4s and taken the record to what Ato Bolden described as "not a time. It sounds like my dad's birth date."

I've heard people say they were surprised by my reaction, my unrestrained joy. I guess I can come across to some people as cold and calculating, unemotional. Well, I believe one of the most important parts of self-control is knowing when to let go of it, when to lie back in the water and just enjoy. My arms flew out, my mouth flew open, and I knelt on the track beside an accomplishment that surprised even me.

Yet it was not some kind of miracle. If I were not capable of doing it, I wouldn't have done it. It was the junction of everything I had done up until that point, the tip of an iceberg of hard work and dedication, of talent and opportunity.

I had done something few people ever get to do, to be the very best—the best ever!—at one thing. But that wasn't the only reason to celebrate.

The other reason was something that anyone can celebrate. It was the pride of accomplishment, the knowledge that I was propelled by every interval I've ever run and every weight I've ever lifted, by every right decision and every time I overcame loss. It was the setting of goals and the devotion to a style of training that worked within the precision of hundredths of seconds. It was the patience and the willingness to chase something relentlessly, even though there were no guarantees I would ever catch it.

It is the thing, finally, that I hope to leave behind. Maybe my legacy will be that I was someone who broke world records and won gold medals and ran faster than anyone had up to that point. Those are things I've always wanted. But I also hope that when other people face their own dragons, they can draw on the lessons and examples I've left behind. I feel like an explorer who has charted some incredible region and leaves his map for anyone who wants to go to the same places I have tried to go.

It is clearly not the journey for everyone. People succeed in as many ways as there are people. Some can be completely fulfilled with destinations that are much closer to home and more comfortable. But if you long to keep going, then I hope you are able to follow my lead to the places I have gone. To within a whisper of your own personal perfection. To places that are sweeter because you worked so hard to arrive there. To places at the very edge of your dreams.

PHOTOGRAPHY CREDITS

page

endpapers © 1991 DUOMO/Paul J. Sutton
ii–iii Reprinted with permission of NIKE, Inc.
vi © Tony Duffy/NBC/Allsport
vii © AP/Wide World Photos
ix © AP/Wide World Photos
xii © Mike Powell/Allsport
xiv © 1995 DUOMO/Paul J. Sutton
xv © 1991 DUOMO/Paul J. Sutton
xv © 1991 DUOMO/Steven E. Sutton
xv © 1995 DUOMO/Steven E. Sutton
xvi–xvii © AP/Wide World Photos
xviii © Tony Duffy/NBC/Allsport
xviii–xix © 1996 DUOMO/Steven E. Sutton
xx © 1996 DUOMO/William R. Sallaz
xxii–xxiii © Mike Powell/Allsport
xxiv © 1996 DUOMO/Steven E. Sutton
2 Courtesy of the author
4 © 1995 DUOMO/Paul J. Sutton
5 Courtesy of the author
6 Courtesy of the author
7 Courtesy of the author
8 © 1996 DUOMO/Steven E. Sutton
11 Courtesy of the author
12 © Tony Duffy/Allsport
14 © 1995 DUOMO/Steven E. Sutton
16–17 © 1992 DUOMO/Paul J. Sutton
17 Courtesy of the author
18–19 © Mike Powell/Allsport
21 © 1995 DUOMO/Paul J. Sutton
22–23 © AP/Wide World Photos
24 © AP/Wide World Photos
27 © 1991 DUOMO/Steven E. Sutton
28 Courtesy of Clyde Hart
31 Courtesy of Clyde Hart
32 Courtesy of the author
35 © Mike Powell/Allsport
36–37 © Bob Martin/Allsport
38 © Gary M. Prior/Allsport
41 © Mike Powell/Allsport
44 © 1996 DUOMO/Steven E. Sutton
47 © AP/Wide World Photos
48 © Photo by DUOMO
50 Mike Powell/Allsport
53 © 1995 DUOMO/Paul J. Sutton
54–55 © AP/Wide World Photos
56–57 © 1993 DUOMO/Paul J. Sutton
56–57 © 1993 DUOMO/Steven E. Sutton
56–57 © 1993 DUOMO/David Madison
59 © Yann Guichaoua/Allsport/Vandystadt
60 © 1995 DUOMO/Steven E. Sutton
62 © 1991 DUOMO/Paul J. Sutton
65 © 1993 DUOMO/Paul J. Sutton
66 © Tony Duffy/Allsport
69 © 1991 DUOMO/Paul J. Sutton
70 © Tony Duffy/Allsport
73 DUOMO
74–75 © 1996 DUOMO/Chris Cole
76 Courtesy of Clyde Hart
79 © Andy Lyons/Allsport
81 Courtesy of Clyde Hart
82 © Göteborg-Tidningen/Jan WiridÇn
84 © 1991 DUOMO/Steven E. Sutton
87 © AP/Wide World Photos
88 © Mike Powell/Allsport
90 © Gary M. Prior/Allsport
93 © 1996 DUOMO/Steven E. Sutton

96–97 © AP/Wide World Photos
98–99 © 1996 DUOMO/Paul J. Sutton
100 Courtesy of Howard L. Bingham
102 © Claus Andersen/Allsport
105 Courtesy of the author
107 © 1991 DUOMO/Paul J. Sutton
108 © 1995 DUOMO/Paul J. Sutton
110 Courtesy of the author
112 © Mike Powell/Allsport
115 © 1992 DUOMO/David Madison
116–17 © 1991 DUOMO/Paul J. Sutton
119 © AP/Wide World Photos
120 © 1995 DUOMO/Steven E. Sutton
123 © 1996 DUOMO/David Madison
124 © 1992 DUOMO/Paul J. Sutton
127 © Mike Powell/Allsport
129 © 1991 DUOMO/Steven E. Sutton
131 © 1996 DUOMO/David Madison
132–33 © 1996 DUOMO/Chris Cole
134 © AP/Wide World Photos
137 © 1991 DUOMO/Paul J. Sutton
138 Courtesy of the author
140 © Gary M. Prior/Allsport
143 © 1992 DUOMO/Paul J. Sutton
144 © 1992 DUOMO/Paul J. Sutton
148 © 1991 DUOMO/Paul J. Sutton
151 Courtesy of the author
153 © 1991 DUOMO/Paul J. Sutton
154 © Mike Powell/Allsport
156 © AP/Wide World Photos
158 © Mike Powell/Allsport
161 © 1993 DUOMO/Paul J. Sutton
163 © 1991 DUOMO/Steven E. Sutton
164 © 1991 DUOMO/Paul J. Sutton
166 © 1995 DUOMO/Steven E. Sutton
169 © 1995 DUOMO/Steven E. Sutton
172 © Clive Brunskill/Allsport
175 © 1995 DUOMO/Paul J. Sutton
177 © Mike Powell/Allsport
178 © AP/Wide World Photos
181 © AP/Wide World Photos
183 © AP/Wide World Photos
184 Courtesy of the author
186 © AP/Wide World Photos
188 © Gary M. Prior/Allsport
191 © 1996 DUOMO/Ben Van Hook
192–93 © SWATCH Timing AG
194 © Webster Riddick
195 © 1996 DUOMO/Chris Cole
199 © 1996 DUOMO/Chris Cole
200–201 © Andy Lyons/Allsport
203 © 1996 DUOMO/Chris Cole
205 © 1996 DUOMO/Chris Cole
206 © SWATCH Timing AG
209 © AP/Wide World Photos
210 © 1995 DUOMO/Steven E. Sutton
213 © Mike Powell/Allsport
215 © 1996 DUOMO/William R. Sallaz
217 © 1996 DUOMO/Chris Cole
219 © 1996 DUOMO/Chris Cole
220 © AP/Wide World Photos
224 © SWATCH Timing AG
226 © Mike Powell/Allsport
227 © 1996 DUOMO/William R. Sallaz
228 © 1996 DUOMO/David Madison
231 ©AP/Wide World Photos

" *T*his is a book about how to identify what you really want and how to get there; to set goals based on realism and confidence; to work with discipline and resolve; to learn from the requisite failures and the too-early successes; to achieve a clarity of focus and a